THE FORBIDDEN CITY IN BEIJING

Compiled by Zheng Zhihai and Qu Zhijing

China Today Press

Executive editor: Qing Xianyou

Editor: Gao ge

Translated by: Gu Shilong, Fu Xukun
and Chen De

Englished edited by: Yang Xianyi, Robert Friend
and Liu Zongren

Photos by: zhang zhao ji   Hu Chui   Wang hui
Lin jing   Liu chen   Yang yin   Zong ren

Layout designer: Zongren

The Forbbiden City in Beijing

Zheng Zhihai and Qu Zhijing

Published by: China Today Press

(24 Baiwanzhuang Road, Beijing, China)

Distributed by: Readers Service

Department, China Tdeay Press

First Edition: 1996

ISBN 7—5072—0630—0/J · 193

Price: 010000

CONTENTS

The Palace Museum

In the year 916 the Liao dynasty established its capital at Beijing, and the city remained the national capital during the Jin, Yuan, Ming and Qing dynasties. Beijing is the largest and best-preserved of China's historic six capital cities.

During the Ming dynasty, the imperial palace in the center of Beijing, also known as the Forbbiden City, took shape as a magnificent architectural complex. Now the Palace Museum, the former palace is famous worldwide for its striking architecture and precious collections of cultural and art objects.

Construction of the palace began in 1406, during the reign of Emperor Yong Le of the Ming dynasty, and was completed in 1420. Over the next 491 years, the palace housed 14 Ming and 10 Qing emperors.

The palace was built on the eight-kilometer south-north axis of Beijing city. Its southern gate, Tian'anmen, faced directly toward the old city gates of Yongding, Zhengyang and Daming. Inside the Tian'anmen were the palace gates of Duan and Wu. The central axis passed through the palace's Outer and Inner Courts. Immediately outside the northern palace gate is Jingshan (Coal Hill). Farther on are the Drum and Bell Towers in the far north of the city. Symmetrically arranged in the four corners of Beijing four temples were located — the Temple of Heaven in the south, of the Earth in the north, of the Sun in the east, and of the Moon in the west. The imperial palace was in the center of the four temples.

The entire palace area, rectangular in shape and 960 meters from north to south and 750 meters from east to west, was surrounded by walls 10 meters high and 3,428 meters long. At each of the four corners of the wall was a tower with nine beams, 18 pillars and 72 roof ridges — a unique design of Chinese traditional architecture. The imperial palace was guarded by 36 battalions and a moat 52 meters wide and 3,800 meters long. The defense was described as impregnable — "a city of bronze with boiling water around it. "

The palace structures themselves covered 720,000 square meters and included more than 9,000 rooms. Construction during the Ming dynasty engaged 100,000 craftsmen and more than one million laborers. The *Nanmu* hardwood came from Sichuan, Guangdong and Yunnan provinces. Renovations during the Qing dynasty used pine wood from northeastern China. The bricks for the walls were made at Linqing in Shandong province, and the square tiles paving the floors came from special Suzhou kilns. Marble slabs were from Fangshan county south of Beijing. Colored stone was from Jixian county, and granite from Quyang county, both in Hebei province. The grand halls are of wood with crimson walls and yellow glazed tile roofs.

The layout is strictly symmetrical. Main halls are on the central axis. Exclusive courtyards of different sizes lie on either side. Imposing and lavishly furnished, the palace symbolized the supreme power of the emperors and illustrated the high workmanship of Chinese architecture.

The palace consists of two complexes, the Outer and the Inner Courts. The main structures of the Outer Court are the Taihedian (Hall of Supreme Harmony), Zhonghedian (Hall of Central Harmony), Baohedian (Hall of Preserving Harmony), and two winghalls; Wenhuadian (Hall of Literary Glory) and Wuyingdian (Hall of the Martial Spirit). The three main halls were where the emperors held official audiences, award ceremonies, weddings, birth celebrations and official banquets. North of the three grand halls is the Inner Court, where the emperor and his family once lived.

Qianqinggong (Palace of Heavenly Purity) was the residence of the emperor. Kunninggong (Palace of Earthly Tranquility) housed the empresses. Between the two palaces is Jiaotaidian (Hall of Union) implying the union of Heaven and Earth. Through the Kunningmen Gate one reaches the imperial gardens, a fine example of traditional Chinese landscaping art.

Artificial rock formations, pavilions, ancient firs and cypresses, flowers and bamboo blend into a harmonious unit.

On both sides of the Inner Court are the Six Eastern and Six Western Palaces, reached through the gates of Rijing, Yuehua, Longguang, Fengeai, Jihua, Duanze, Jinghe and Longfu. Each of the two palace groups contains two courtyards divided into a front hall where audiences were held, bedrooms and wing rooms. The courtyards are connected by neatly designed lanes and corridors. The Six Western Palaces are named Yongshougong (Palace of Longevity), Taijidian (Hall of Supremacy), Yikungong (Palace of the Queen Consort), Changchungong (Palace of Eternal Spring), Chuxiugong (Palace for Gathering Elegance) ajd Jianfugong (Palace of Retaining Happiness). The Yangxingian (Hall of Mental Cultivation) south of the Six Western Palaces was where Qing emperors from Yong Zheng to Xuan Tong lived and handled state affairs.

The six Eastern Palaces are named Jingrengong (Palace of Great Benevolence), Chengqiangong (Palace of Inheriting from Heaven), Zhongcuigong (Palace of Quintessence), Yanxigong (Palace of Prolonging Happiness), Yonghegong (Palace of Eternal Harmony) and Jingyanggong (Palace of Great Brilliance). South of the Six Eastern Palaces is a palace wher emperors fasted. At the rear of either the Eastern or Western Palaces are five groups of identical buildings where the sons of the emperor lived.

On the westernmost edge of the Forbbiden City, commonly known as the Western Outer Palaces, are theCininggong (Palace of Motherly Tranquility) and Shoukanggong (Palace of Health), which served as residences for dowager empresses and imperial consorts of an older generation. On the easternmost edge inside the Forbbiden City, commonly known as the Eastern Outer Palaces, are the Huangjidian (Hall of Imperial Supremacy) and the Ningshougong (Palace of Tranquil Longevity), built especially by the Qing emperor Qian Long for himself before his abdication.

The Forbbiden City is not only the center of Beijing but also one of the city's best scenic spots. On its northwest are the Taiyechi (Imperial Water Pond) and Qionghua Isle, an imperial lodging during the Liao and Jin dynasties. On its west is Zhongnanhai (Central South Sea). Jingshan Hill to the north forms a natural screen for the imperial palace. Jinshuihe (Gold Water River), an artificial stream, flows in front of the southern palace gate. From Wanchunting (Pavilion of 10, 000 Springs) on top of Jingshan Hill one can overlook the whole Forbbiden City — a sea of grand dark red buildings with golden roofs.

The 1911 revolution overthrew the Qing dynasty, ending over 2,000 years of feudal rule in China. But the last emperor, Aisin-Gioro Pu Yi, stayed on in the Inner Court for another 13 years. On November 5, 1924, Lu Zhonglin, an army commander under General Feng Yuxiang, chased him out. On October 10, 1925, the former imperial palace became a museum.

The largest museum in China, the Palace Museum houses over a million paintings, objets d'art made of jade, gold and silver, and other cultural and art treasures. After the founding of the People's Republic of China in 1949, the government sponsored much-needed, large-scale renovations of the museum, sorted out great numbers of cultural relics and put them on display. Today the grand halls in the Outer Court, the Inner Court, the Yangxindian and the Six Western Palaces contain objects from the different centuries of imperial rule. Baohedian and the rooms on the two wings display artistic pieces. There are nine other exhibition halls featuring bronzes, porcelains, handicrafts of the Ming and Qing dynasties, and paintings. Most tourists like to begin their tour from the southern gate of Tian'anmen, which has been called the "National Gate of China." Many visitors feel they have not really been to Beijing unless they can see the former palace.

A General
Introduction to
the Forbbiden City

Beijing is a great metropolis with a long history. In 938 it became the second capital of the Liao dynasty. Since then, the city had been the capital of the Jin, Yuan, Ming and Qing dynasties over a span of more than 1,000 years.

In Beijing, the most magnificent architectural complex is the Forbidden City in the heart of the city. Here the grand halls and high buildings manifesting the Chinese ancient styles are the best-preserved palace structures left trom the feudal dynasties.

The Forbidden City was the Imperial Palace of the Ming and Qing dynasties. during a long period of 491 years from 1420, when Yong Le, the third emperor of the Ming dynasty, moved the capital from Nanjing to Beijing, down to 1911, when Pu Yi, the last emperor of the Qing dynasty, was overthrown, 24 emperors (14 of the Ming and 10 of the Qing) lived inside and ruled the nation with an absolute authority rarely paralleled in human history.

The palace grounds are divided into two sections—the Outer Court and the Inner Court. The Outer Court centers around three big halls (the Hall of Supreme Harmony, the Hall of Middle Harmony and the Hall of Preserving Harmony) with the Hall of Literary Glory and the Hall of Martial Spirit on two sides. It is the place where the emperor issued imperial decrees or conducted important state ceremonies. Behind the Outer Court is the Inner Court, where are located the three rear palaces (the Palace of Heavenly Purity, the Hall of Union and the Palace of Earthly Tranquility), the Imperial Gar-

den, Six Eastern and Six Western Palaces. In addition to those, there are the Hall of Imperial Supremacy and the Palace of Tranquil Longevity in the east and the Palace of Motherly Tranquility in the west. The emperor handled state affairs in the Inner Court and also lived there with his family.

In 1913 the three big halls in the Outer Court, the Hall of Literary Glory and the Hall of Martial Spirit were converted into exhibition halls, where cultural relics and art treasures brought from the old palace in Shenyang and the Summer Palace in Chengde were put on display. On October10, 1925, the rear part of the Forbidden City was open to the public. In 1947 the Palace Museum was formally established.

After the founding of the People's Republic of China in 1949, the government sponsored large-scale renovations of this ancient architectural complex, which has taken on a new look since then. From 1952 to 1958, 250,000 cubic meters of garbage, left from the days of the Ming and Qing dynasties as well as the KMT rule, was removed out of the palace grounds; the sewer system built in the Ming and Qing times was dredged; lightening rods were installed on main buildings. Apart from these, great numbers of cultural relics were sorted out and put on systematic show. Today the grand halls in the Outer Court, the three Rear Palaces, the Hall of Mental Cultivation and the Six Western Palaces are open to visitors, who can have a look at the decorations and the art objects from different centuries of the imperial rule. The Six Eastern Palaces

have been turned into exhibition halls featuring bronze, porcelains, handicrafts of the Ming and Qing dynasties. The rooms on the two wings of the three big front halls now display artistic pieces from various periods of Chinese history. The Hall of Imperial Supremacy is devoted to the show of old paintings. There is a permanent exhibition of palace treasures in the Hall of Cultivating Nature, the Hall of Joyful Longevity and the Hall of Sustained Harmony.

In 1961 the State Council designated the former imperial palace as one of the key historic monuments under national protection.

Palace Museum, the largest one in China, receives seven to eight million visitors annually. Since 1949 tourists from more than 160 countries and regions have visited this place.

Construction of the Forbidden City

In 1403 Zhu Di, the fourth son of the founder of the Ming dynasty, mounted the throne in Nanjing after driving his nephew, the second emperor, out of the palace at the end of a four-year-old civil war. Since he had already built up his power base in Beijing, the first imperial decree Zhu Di issued after he came into power was to move the capital from Nanjing to Beijing. Besides, he fully understood that the remaining forces of the overthrown Yuan dynasty were not reconciled to their defeat and had always planned to come back. To relieve this dire threat to the Ming dynasty, he made Beijing the capital.

Construction of the Imperial Palace began in 1406 at the order of Emperor Yong Le (Zhu Di). As many as one million conscripted labourers and craftsmen from various provinces came in rotation to work for this grandiose project.

The timber used for building the palace was brought from Sichuan, Jiangxi, Zhejiang, Shanxi and Hunan provinces. Transportation of timber was extremely difficult in those days. In Sichuan province the logs cut down had to be left in the mountains, waiting for mountain torrents to wash them into rivers, and then shipped to Beijing through the Grand Canal. Such shipment was very costly. For example, during the reign of Wan Li, it cost 9.3 million taels of silver to transport the timber for the reconstruction of the three big halls in the Outer Court.

Most of the stones used for building the palace were quarried from the suburban county of Fangshan. To transport some huge stones was even more difficult. According to historical records, 20,000 peasants were employ-ed to move an immense piece of stone, 10 meters long, 3 meters wide and 1.6 meters thick, over an ice-path made by pouring water on the road in severe winter. The massive stone block reached Beijing in 28 days after being pulled by thousands of horses and mules.

The bricks were made in Linqing, Shandong province, and over 10 million bricks were required for the construction of the Forbidden City. In the reign of Yong Le, there were 384 kilns in Linqing, and one million bricks were turned out every year. The floors of all the buildings in the Forbidden City were paved with square tiles, which required more than 20 steps to finish and then were immersed in tung oil for a permanent polish. The making of each square tile took a whole year. They were made in special kilns in south China, 2,000 kilometers away, and were shipped to Beijing by boats.

In the Forbidden City all the walls are crimson in color, because it denotes dignity and solemnity. The tiles on the roof are mostly yellow in colour, for it stands for the "center" in the ancient Chinese philosophy. However, the roof of the princes' residences was green, because they were inferior in rank. The Pavilion of the Source of Literature (Wenyuange), a royal library, was roofed with black tiles so as to prevent fire, because black color symbolized water in the ancient times. All the glazed tiles for the buildings in the Forbidden City were made in the western suburbs of Beijing.

The Forbidden City was built after the imperial palace in Nanjing on the old site of the palace of the Yuan dynasty, but the exact location was moved about 400 meters to the south.

In 1420 the Forbidden City was basically completed. It occupied an area of 720,000 square meters, with nearly 100 courtyards and more than 9,000 rooms (now 8,600 rooms or so are still standing). The total floor space amounted to 160,000 square meters. The entire palace area, rectangular in shape, 960 meters from north to south and 750 meters from east to west, was surrounded by walls, 10 meters high and 3,428 meters long. There is a gate on each side: Meridian Gate in the south; East Flowery Gate in the east; West Flowery Gate in the west and the Gate of Divine Prowess in the north. At each of the four corners of the Forbidden City stands a corner-tower with 9 beams, 18 pillars and 72 roof ridges—a unique design of Chinese traditional architecture. Around the Forbidden City there is a moat, named Outer Golden Water River, 52 meters wide and 3,800 meters long. The water in the moat used to come from Jade Spring Hill in the western suburbs of Beijing. Besides, there is an inner moat, named Inner Golden Water River, winding around inside the Forbidden City. In addition to being one of the important fortifications of the palace, Golden Water River not only provided water for fire-prevention, but also served as a main drainage ditch.

Vicinity of the Forbidden City

The Forbidden City stands on the 8-kilometer-long central axis of the capital, running from Yongding Gate in the south to the Bell and Drum Towers in the north. The central axis at that time passed through Zhengyang Gate, Daming Gate (Daqing Gate in the Qing dynasty), Tian'anmen Gate, Upright Gate, Meridian Gate, the Outer Court and the Inner

Court of the Imperial Palace and then the Coal Hill.

To the east of the Forbidden City stood the Imperial Ancestral Temple, where the emperor worshipped his ancestors. To the west lay the Altar of Land and Grain, which was sectioned and filled with earth in five different colours to symbolize that all land belonged to the emperor. Besides, four temples were symmetrically located in the four sides out of the city: the Temple of Heaven in the south, of the Earth in the north, of the Sun in the east, and of the Moon in the west, with the Forbidden City in the center.

Between Zhengyang City Gate and the Meridian Gate, the main entrance to the Forbidden City, was an one-kilometer-long thoroughfare, running through three high gatetowers and a few squares of different sizes. On both sides of the thoroughfare were buildings that housed various government ministries and military headquarters, which served as an outpost area for the Forbidden City.

West of the Forbidden City is Zhongnanhai (Middle and Southern Sea) and northwest is Beihai (Northern Sea) with an island called Qionghuadao, which was the pleasure palace in the Liao and Jin dynasties. To the north lies Coal Hill, because coal used to be stored there in the early Ming times. During the reign of Yong Le, an artificial hill was built on this site by heaping up the garbage from the construction of the Forbidden City and the earth excavated in digging the moat and Zhongnanhai. The hill is about one kilometer in circumference with a 44.6-meter-high peak, the highest point of the old city of Beijing. Since the Golden Water River flows south of the Imperial Palace, the whole lay-out is in complete accordance with the traditional architectural pattern that the royal palace complex must have a green river flowing in front and a lush hill lying at the back.

Outside the Forbidden City stood the Imperial City Wall, which used to be the surrounding wall of the Yuan Palace. Inside the Imperial City there were 24 government office buildings in the Ming dynasty and 13 in the Qing dynasty in addition to more palace structures. It was out of bounds to ordinary citizens.

The Forbidden City was protected by three high city walls (the Forbidden City Wall, the Imperial City Wall and the Beijing City Wall), which made the Imperial Palace unassailable through centuries.

Five Gates to
the Forbbiden City

There are five gates to the Forbidden City, one after the other. In ancient times, as early as the Zhou dynasty, it was an established rule for the emperor to have five gates to his palace. This age-old practice was also followed by the Ming and Qing emperors. All the officials who went to attend grand ceremonies had to pass through five gates: Daqing Gate (Daming Gate in the Ming Dynasty), the Gate of Heavenly Peace, Upright Gate, Meridian Gate (the main entrance to the Forbidden City) and the Gate of Supreme Harmony.

If Yongding Gate of the Outer City, Zhengyang Gate of the Inner City, the Arrow Castle (commonly known as the Front Gate) and the Gate of Heavenly Purity, the main gate to the Inner Court, were also included, it came to a total of nine gates, which again signifies the supremacy of the emperor.

Gate of Great Qing (Daqingmen)

In was originally called Daming Gate (the Gate of Great Ming) in the Ming dynasty and renamed Zhonghua Gate (the Gate of China) after the 1911 Revolution. Now it is no longer in existence.

This gate was situated to the north of Zhengyang City Gate, and in between was the Heavenly Street, a flourishing market street in the old days.

Only the empress dowager and the emperor had free passage through these three main gates in the Imperial City, i.e.

Daqing Gate, the Gate of Heavenly Peace and Upright Gate. The empress had this privilege only once in her lifetime. She was carried through the three gates on her wedding day.

In the Ming times, between this gate and the Gate of Heavenly Peace was a covered corridor flanked on two sides by 144 connected office rooms. Here the Ministry of Interior and the Ministry of Defense selected officials, and the Board of Rites reviewed and finalized the test-paper for the imperial examination. The Ministry of Justice carried out "Autumn Sentence" there in the middle of the 8th lunar month every year. In the 5th lunar month, the files of all the convicts under sentences of death from various provinces were sorted out and put into seperate books, which would be presented to the emperor in the early 7th lunar month. In the middle of the 8th lunar month, the emperor would give his judgment on the death sentences after conferring with his ministers. Those whose death sentence was reversed were met at the gate by their relatives who would put a string of crabapples around their necks to celebrate their good luck.

Farther south were more buildings that housed various government departments.

Gate of Heavenly Peace (Tian'anmen)

It was first built in the Ming dynasty and rebuilt in 1651 under the reign of

Shun Zhi, the third emperor of the Qing dynasty.

The gate-tower is 33.7 meters high with 60 red pillars and 36 windows open to the south. The whole building occupies an area of more than 20,000 square meters and is noted for its double eaves and the hipped roof with nine ridges and ten glazed pottery dragons on top. In the Ming and Qing times, the emperor was always carried through this gate when he went to the Temple of Heaven, of Earth and of Agriculture. In case the emperor had to lead the army personally in an expedition, he would offer sacrifices to gods in front of this gate. If it was the general who was to command the expedition, the emperor would come to see him off at this gate.

The ceremony of issuing imperial edicts was held here on important official occasions. During the ceremony the officials would kneel south of the Gold Water Bridge and bow to the north while the Commissioner read out the imperial edict. When this was over, the Commissioner would roll the edict and put it in the mouth of a wooden, gold-painted phoenix, which was tied to a yellow rope. Then the Commissioner would slowly lower down the phoenix with the edict and the officials from the Board of Rites would receive the edict in a wooden tray shaped like a cloudlet. The edict would be afterwards taken to the Board of Rites, where copies on yellow paper were made by hand for dispatch to the whole country. This was known as "the Imperial Edicts Delivered by Gold Phoenix".

Tian'anmen Gate was also called "the

State Gate" with a pair of Huabiao (ornamental pillars) both in front of and behind it. Besides, there are five marble bridges spanning the outer moat before the gate. The central bridge was reserved for the exclusive passage of the emperor's palanquin. The next two bridges were for the princes and dukes, and the bridges at the far ends were for the officials with ranks.

Between Tian'anmen Gate and Upright Gate were 26 office rooms spread on both sides of the central passageway. On the west side used to be the office for the Board of Public Works and on the east the office for the Board of Rites.

Upright Gate
(Duanmen)

This gate is identical with the Gate of Heavenly Peace (Tian'anmen) both in design and in structure. The imposing gate-towers add much solemnity to the Forbidden City.

Between Upright Gate and Meridian Gate were 42 office rooms occupied by various ministries and imperial boards. Beyond the office rooms there were three meeting rooms on each side, where the princes and ministers met before an official audience.

Meridian Gate
(Wumen)

It is the largest gate of the Forbidden City and stands on the central axis of the capital. The emperor believed that the meridian passed through this gate, hence its name. The entire structure is shaped like the letter U. There are three openings in the middle and one sidegate on each side. Beyond the gate is a square, 9,900 square meters in area. Surmounted by five pavilions, this massive gate is also known as the "Five-Phoenix Tower". The main pavilion in the middle, nine bays wide and five bays deep, is topped by a double-eaved hipped roof. The two square double-eaved pavilions on either side, connected by covered corridors, serve as eastern and western wings of the pavilion. Drums and bells were installed in the side pavilions. When the emperor went to the royal temples to attend sacrificial rites, the bells were struck to mark this important occasion. When he went to the Ancestral Temple, it was known to the public by beating the drums. During the grand ceremony held in the Hall of Supreme Harmony both the bells and the drums were sounded.

In the Ming times, lanterns were hung over this gate on the 15th of the first lunar month. A brilliant banquet was given by the emperor in the top pavilions to entertain ministers and other high-ranking officials. During the banquet the emperor would compose a poem and then order some officials to write another poem using same rhyme-words as his. On the day of a grand ceremony or an imperial audience, all the officials began to wait outside Meridian Gate before daybreak. When the drums were beaten for the first time, the officials would line up in order of ranks. When the drums were beaten for the second time, the officials from the Board of Rites would come and guide those waiting officials into the palace through the two sidegates. When the drums were beaten for the third time, the emperor would ascend the throne. In those days this gate was also the place to punish high officials who had offended the emperor. They would be clubbed near the east wing of the gate.

Meridian Gate has five openings. The central one was used exclusively by the emperor. The empress could enter the palace through this gate only on the day of her wedding.

On the day when the successful candidates of the imperial examination were announced, the number one, number two and number three were allowed to pass through the central opening. The princes and dukes were supposed to use the opening to the west, and the ministers the one to the east. Those who came to the capital for the "Palace Examination", the highest level of the nationwide imperial examination system, were guided into the Forbidden City through two sidegates.

This gate was heavily guarded in the old days. Two guards were seated in front of the gate, red cudgels in hand. They usually did not have to get up except when a prince was passing through. Anyone who attempted to enter without presenting himself first, would be cudgelled by the guards.

Beyond Meridian Gate is a large courtyard, traversed by the Inner Golden Water River, which flows east like a belt of jade. Five marble bridges (commonly known as Jade Belt Bridges) crossing the river, lead to the Gate of Supreme Harmony.

Gate of Supreme Harmony (Taihemen)

Built in the Ming dynasty, it was first called the Gate of Obeying the Heaven, and then renamed in the Qing dynasty. This gate was the main entrance to the Outer Court and the most important gate within the Forbidden City.

In the Ming dynasty the emperor sometimes held court at this gate. In the Qing dynasty, when the emperor went to the royal temples, he always changed to a large-sized palanquin here. On the occasion of a grand ceremony an orchestra would be spread out along the north veranda of this gate. Beside this main gate there is one sidegate on the east and west. For a grand ceremony the civil officials entered the huge courtyard of the Hall of Supreme Harmony through the east sidegate and the millitary officials and foreign envoys through the west sidegate.

In the Ming times, there were 48 rooms on both sides of this gate.

Those on the east were chronicler's office, where court records and genealogy of the royal house were kept. Those on the west were classrooms for the princes and the office for compiling books on institutions and laws.

Southeast of the Gate of Supreme Harmony stands Xiehe Gate. To its north was the office in charge of checking the implementation of emperor's edicts. To its south was the office in charge of commending the officials with meritorious deeds and granting ranks of nobility. Southwest of the gate is Xohe Gate. To its north was the office for translaters whose job was translating official documents and the imperial edicts from Manchu into Han or vice versa. In 1650 *Water Margin*, one of the best-known Chinese classics, was translated into Manchu in this place. To its south was the office for the officials in charge of taking down the emperor's words and actions everyday. Such records would be sent to the Cabinet at the end of every year, and then put in the Royal Archives under the supervision of the ministers.

Outer Court—
Ground for
Ceremonial Occasions

Beyond the Gate of Supreme Harmony is the spacious courtyard of the Hall of Supreme Harmony which measures over 30,000 square meters in area. In the middle is the "Imperial Pathway" paved with large flagstones and the whole area other than this is paved with bricks. On both sides there are over 100 stone pedestals, arranged in diagonal lines, embeded in the ground to mark the positions of ceremonial paraphernalia, such as flags, weapons, shields, parasols, fans, gold and silver decorations, etc, displayed on ceremonies marking important occasions. Civilian and military officials of different ranks attending ceremonies had to kneel down along the Imperial Pathway in order of precedence at designated places marked by bronze "rank markers" which total 72 for 18 ranks. Civilian officials took their places on the east side and military officials on the west. Even foreign envoys, when watching the ceremony, had to do the same at a place specially reserved for them. At the east and west ends of this cloistered courtyard are two side halls, both 25 meters high called Tirenge and Hongyige.

The Hall of Supreme Harmony and two other main halls of the Outer Court stand on a vast three-tiered marble terrace which is 8.13 meters high and edged with finely carved balustrades on each tier. There are altogether 1,458 white marble balusters carved with patterns of dragons and phoenixes. At the base of these balustrades are a great number of gargoyles in the shape of dragon head which make a spectacle during a downpour.

Hall of Supreme Harmony (Taihedian)

It is popularly referred to as "the Hall of Gold Throne". In the Ming dynasty it was originally called "the Hall of Veneration of Heaven" when it was first built and was changed to "the Hall of Imperial Supremacy" in 1563. It was changed to the present name in the Qing dynasty to signify universal harmony. The hall has a floor space of 2,377 square meters with 72 pillars standing in six rows. The traditional way of calculating the space of a building is to count the square enclosed by four pillars as one "room", so this hall can be said to have 55 "rooms". The height of the pillars at the wall is 12.7 meters and the diameter of each is 1.06 meters. This hall had been rebuilt for seven times, the last one being from 1695 to 1697 in the reign of Emperor Kang Xi. The designer Liangjiu was an architect serving in the Ministry of Engineering. He made a maquette and had all the parts made and assembled according to it. The structure and technology proved to be perfect with over 10,000 well-fitting parts and details. In the feudal society buildings were differentiated by different roof-style and decoration as their owners deffered in official ranks or social status. So the roof is, in this case, the double tiered Wudian hipped-roof style. The hall stands 35.05 meters high (37.44 meters including the rooftop decoration — liwen). It is the biggest ancient wood structure extant in China.

In the middle of the hall stand six gilded columns carved with coiled dragons. In the space enclosed by these six columns is the gilded imperial throne placed on a dais two meters high. Behind the throne is a carved screen. On either side of the throne are a crane-shaped candlestick, an elephant-shaped incense burner, a column-shaped incense burner with a pagoda top and a luduan (a mythical beast) which are all cloisonne wares.

Elephant carrying a vase filled with grains is a symbol of peace and prosperity in China. Luduan, the mythical beast, is said to be capable of travelling 9,000 kilometers a day and understanding all kinds of languages in the world. It would only appear in the reign of a virtuous emperor, always keeping close watch on him by his side. Very eccentric in shape, it looks like a square block with a unicorned head facing upward. Its four legs are entwined by a snake. Snake is the totem of the wife of the legendary Yellow Emperor. The crane is a symbol of longevity, supposed to have a life span of 10,000 years. There are clockworks in this pair of cranes to make the wings beat. It is a favorite mascot of the feudal rulers for they wished to live long and retain their dynasties. there are four other incense burners in front of the dais in the shape of elephant head with three legs. On a ceremony all these incense burners would burn sandalwood, giving out fragrant smoke.

Above the throne is a gilded coffered ceiling with a dragon-phoenix pattern. Hanging underneath are glass balls called "Mirrors of the Yellow Emperor" which represent orthodox succession. In the

Ming dynasty there was a screen of woven thread of copper in front of the throne.

There were 24 emperors enthroned in Beijing during the Ming and Qing dynasties. All the enthronement ceremonies were held in this hall. On such an occasion an enthronement edict was proclaimed and homage was paid and congratulations were offered by the attending oficials and noblemen. Other grand ceremonies were also held here on such occasions as New Year's Day, Winter Solstice, Longevity Festival, proclamation of imperial edicts, the enthronement of the empress, receiving successful candidates of the imperial examination, appointment of commander-in-chief of expedition troops during a war.

When the last emperor of the Qing dynasty, Aisin Gioro Pu Yi was enthroned in this hall on December 2, 1908, he was only a child of three. While the ceremony was going on the boy emperor became fidgeting and kept crying. His father, Prince Regent Zaifeng, was kneeling below the throne and supporting him on the throne. As the boy emperor kept crying: "I don't like it here. I want to go home." He tried to soothe him by saying: "Don't cry. It'll soon be over." After the ceremony, officials in their surreptitious gossip took these words as an evil omen. By coincidence, these words proved to be prophetic, as within three years, the Qing dynasty was finished.

Not long after the Revolution of 1911, Yuan Shikai usurped state power and enthroned himself as Emperor Hong Xian on December 12, 1915. He had the hall refurbished for the occasion, changing all the billingual (Han and Manchu) inscriptions into the Han language. Yuan changed the name of the hall into Chengyuandian. For fear that the glass balls might drop and injure him, he had the dais and the throne moved backwards to where it is now. He replaced the throne with a new one specially made to suit his short legs. The new throne had short legs but high back to give an imposing impression. In appearance it was a mixture of Chinese and Western styles. The coup immediately incurred opposition from allover the country. Guizhou, Guangdong, Guangxi, Fujian, Zhejiang and Shaanxi provinces declared independant succesively. The regime lasted only 80 days, ending with Yuan's death.

The throne on display now is the original one of the Ming dynasty. It was discovered in the imperial stock in 1959.

During the Ming and Qing dynasties the floor was covered with yellow carpet lined with palm and rush mats. The dais was also covered with a piece of embroidered cloth patterned with coiled dragons.

On a grand ceremony, two Ministers of the Presence stood by the side when the emperor mounted the throne. Ten Companions of the Presence and ten guards carrying swords flanked the space in front of the throne. Behind the throne stood ten Rear Attendants carrying Leopard Tail lances. By the column to the east of the throne was a table for the imperial seals; by the column to the west of the throne was a table for decrees. By the column behind that one were seated two Imperial Chroniclers. A table for letters of congratulations and benedictions was placed on the eastern side outside the door. On both sides of Danbi (Red Stairway, referring to the middle space right in front of the hall) there were tables for articles of tribute from foreign countries.

Outside the hall, at the east side of the porch stood academicians of different ranks and at the west side stood princes and censors of different ranks. At the east end of the porch was placed a chime of golden bells and at the west end a set of jade qing (a kind of percussion instrument) and other musical instruments including heng, flute, zither, etc. The band called Middle Harmony Superior Music played as the emperor mounted the throne. When the music ended, four Masters of Ceremony, standing in the courtyard below ordered the men to crack long silk whips for three times and everybody to fall in. In this way the ceremony started, with the band at the Gate of Supreme Harmony, playing Danbi Grand Music and everybody shouting "Longevity". Clouds of incense rose from the bronze cranes and tortoises and the eighteen tripods on the terraces. In such an aura of majesty and mystique the emperor emerged. A very large Guard of Honor stood in line on both sides, extending way down south through the Meridian Gate to beyond the Gate of Heavenly Peace. There were altogether 1,709 men engaged: 66 outside the Hall of Supreme Harmony; 1,063 in the courtyard; 417 outside the Meridian Gate; 31 outside the Gate of Heavenly Peace. The number exceeded 3,000 in the reign of Emperor Kang Xi. In the Hall of

Supreme Harmony 132 Managing Officials tended the rituals. Apart from these, forming part of the pomp were a number of sedan chairs outside the hall, 100 horses in the courtyard, and chariots and elephants carrying vases outside the Meridian Gate.

In the Qing dynasty all the banquets at the Hall of Supreme Harmony were handled by the Board of Rites, with all the provisions supplied by Guanglusi and the food prepared by the Culinary Bureau. Such banquets were held on New Year's Day, Winter Solstice, Longevity Day, Decennial National Day and the Grand Nuptial. There were 108 tables inside the hall: one for the emperor, 49 tables in seven rows on each side for princes and high officials, four tables for Companions of the Presence, and five tables for Rear Attendants and guards. It came to 284 tables including those outside the hall. The banqueters were served either Manchu dishes or Han dishes. Among everything else, over a hundred lambs were consumed on a single banquet.

In the reign of Emperor Kang Xi a Manchu-Han mixed style table offered over a hundred and ten different dishes. They were stacked up one upon the other on one table, not a single dish to be taken away until after the banquet. The stack was arranged in such a way to allow the banqueter easy access to every dish with chopsticks.

Dances were performed after the dinner on the terrace in front of the hall. Officials from the Board of Rites led the dancers to perform a "gallant dance" first— "In Praise of Heroes". Eight officials on prop horses, wearing suits of armor, played the warriors. They carried on their back flags in the colors of the "Eight Banners" to represent Manchu heroes. Another eight performers made up as beasts of prey kept attacking them but were at last killed by their arrows. It was followed by another dance, a "gentle dance"— "Rise for Joy". It was joined by princes, high officials, guards — 40 of them in two lines, facing each other. They danced to the singing of the people by the side. When the dance was over, Mongol music was presented inside the hall with acrobatics played by Koreans and Muslims outside.

During the Ming and Qing dynasties, the outcome of the Civil Service Examinations was announced at the Hall of Supreme Harmony in the presence of the emperor.

Hall of Middle Harmony (Zhonghedian)

It was originally called the Hall of Canopy and changed to the Hall of Middle Supremacy in 1562. In 1645 it was changed to the present name. The origin of the name was found in the *Book of Change*. It means that we should not go extremes, stick to the gold mean and keep in control so that we can reach harmony with everything.

The hall is square with a pyramidic roof. Before his attendance at a cermony in the Hall of Supreme Harmony the emperor would take a short rest in this hall and receive the obeisances of the palace guards, officials from the Inner Cabinet, the Board of Rites, Court of Censors, Hanlin Academy and Imperial Superintendant of Instruction. Every year the emperor would go to Temple of Heaven on summer solstice, Temple of Earth on winter solstice, Temple of Sun on vernal eqinox, Temple of Moon on autumnal eqinox and to Altar of Land and Grain on the eighth month of lunar calendar for worshipping. Before leaving for the worshipping the emperor would examine the ritual address here. On every second month of lunar calendar the emperor would go to the Temple of Agriculture to perform Plowing Ceremony. Before leaving for the ceremony he would check the seeds, plow-shares and other implements and also the ritual address in this hall. The emperor, princes and high officials participating all put their hands to the plows during the ceremony. The emperor would perform ox-leading in plowing while 24 petty officers carrying colored flags with tinkling bells and 36 people singing followed him on both sides. This event would be made known to the whole country by a decree.

The imperial family tree was renewed every ten years. A ceremony was held in this hall to present the renewed family tree, which was called Jade Tablet, to the emperor. The dead was recorded in black and the living in red. The record of the lineage directly related to the emperors had a yellow cover and that of the lateral branches had a red cover. Each record had three copies which were taken to the Imperial Archives, the Clan Register Office in Beijing and the Old Palace in

Shenyang respectively for keeping after the ceremony.

The two sedan chairs on display in this hall date back to the reign of Emperor Qian Long in the 18th century. One is painted black and the other multicolor. Both have painted patterns of dragon-cloud. Each one needed eight people to carry. When a ceremony was to be held in the Hall of Supreme Harmony, the emperor used to mount a sedan chair in front of Qianqingmen (Gate of Heavenly Purity) and be carried to this hall. After a short rest he would step into the Hall of Supreme Harmony from behind.

Hall of Preserving Harmony (Baohedian)

It was originally called the Hall of Discretion and was changed to the Hall of Established Supremacy in 1562. It did not get its present name until the Qing dynasty. The name "Preserving Harmony" has its origin in the *Book of Change*. The building has a double-tiered hip-and-gable (xieshan) roof.

In the Ming dynasty, before going to the ceremony in celebration of granting title on the empress or the crown prince, the emperor would change into full ceremonial dress in this hall.

In the Qing dynasty, the emperor gave banquet in honor of the newly-married son-in-law of his in this hall. The Middle Harmony Superior Music Band was arrayed in front of this hall and the Danbi Grand Music Band behind the Hall of Middle Harmony. A shed with yellow covering was erected between the two halls for heating food. On the first and fifteenth day of the first month of the lunar calendar banquets were given by the emperor in honor of Mongol and Xinjiang nobles, attended by many officials and guards. The expenses on banquets held in this hall were tremendous, especially in the Qing dynasty. For instance, in 1903, 10,227 lambs were consumed on banquets held in this hall, while the total number of lambs consumed in the whole palace was 36,147 for that year.

When the compilation of *A Collection of Imperial Remarks* was finished, it was presented to the emperor in this hall before it was taken to the Imperial Archives for keeping.

From 1789 onward the final session of the Civil Service Examinations was held in this hall with the supervision of the emperor.

The Qing Court attached great importance to the Civil Service Examintions. Eight Evaluation Officials were appointed by the emperor. All the papers were sealed before evaluation. Each of the evaluation officials would mark the papers with a circle if he considered it good. So the best papers may have had eight circles. The best ten papers were presented to the emperor for final decision. The ten successful candidates would be given an audience by the emperor. The three top candidates, besides the titles conferred on them, were given posts of Hanlin Academecians. The rest of the successful candidates had to pass another examina-tion at the Hall of Preserving Harmony so as to be given official posts.

The side chambers of the three main halls of the Outer Court have 33 "rooms" on each side. The east side has the Pavilion of Manifest Benevolence (Tirenge) in the middle. In the Ming dynasty it housed the *Yongle Encyclopaedia*, the biggest of its kind in the world then. It is composed of 22,877 sections of texts and 60 sections of introduction and catalogue. It was bound into 11,099 volumes. In the beginning of the Qing dynasty, the suits of armor of the first few emperors were kept here. During the reign of Emperor Kang Xi, a special examination was held in this hall to supplement the regular ones. But this hall was turned into a storeroom for brocades in the reign Emperor Qian Long. All the other rooms had always been storerooms for armors, saddles and felt goods.

The rooms on the west side, as well as those on the east, were all storerooms of the Household Department. They were for fur and leather, tea, porcelainware, clothing and bronze-ware. The one in the middle was the Treasury (Hongyige — Pavilion of Broad Righteousness).

Two Wings of the Outer Court

The three main halls with side chambers constitute the center of the Outer Court. It is flanked by two groups of buildings on the two wings—represented by the Hall of Literary Glory on the east and the Hall of Military Excellence on the west. The three groups of buildings form the magnificent Outer Court.

Hall of Literary Glory (Wenhuage)

It was built in 1420 as the study for the crown prince, for this it had a green glazed-tile roof. The color of the roof was changed into yellow when it was refurbished in 1522. From then on the emperor used it as an abode for abstinence. Occasionally he would receive high officials here. In the Ming dynasty the papers of civil service examination were presented to the emperor in this hall two days after the final session at the Hall of Preserved Harmony. The placing of the papers which had been evaluated had to be approved by the emperor. He would fix a circle in red ink on each of the papers of the first three places as his final decision. This hall was also the place where Imperial Lecture/Banquets were held in the Ming and Qing dynasties. At first there were no fixed dates for these. They began to be held regularly three times a month at the beginning of the period of Zhengtong of the Ming dynasty, except in the hot and cold months. In 1685 Emperor Kang Xi set the eighth of the second month of the lunar calendar every year as the date for Lecture/Banquet, with eight Manchu and eight Han high officials as lecturers. In the Ming dynasty, sacrifices were offered to emperors of various dynasties in the past on the previous day of the occasion. In the Qing dynasty, sacrifices were offered to Confucious instead. Afterwards the Lecture/Banquets were given at the Concord Gate to the east of the hall or in the side chambers of the hall. Beginning in 1782, the site was moved to the Pavilion of the Source of Literature (Wenyuange).

Hall of Hereditary Soul (Chuanxindian)

It stands in a courtyard to the east of the Hall of Literary Glory for housing the memorial tablets of the first few legendary and historical sovereigns of ancient China (that is, the three august ones, the five sovereigns, and the sage emperors of the three royal dynasties), Confucius and the Duke of Zhou. To the east of the courtyard there is a well famous for its water of natural sweetness. Of the 72 wells in the Forbidden City this in the best. Beiginning in 1652 the Qing Court offered sacrifices to the God of Well here every year. The emperor, nevertheless, did not drink from this well. He had water carted from the Jade Spring in the western suburb for his own use because it was considered superior to this well.

Pavilion of the Source of Literature (Wenyuange)

Located behind the Hall of Literary Glory, it used to be the imperial library. Built in 1774 in the style of Tianyige Pavilion in Ningbo, Zhejiang province, it housed the famous collections: *Siku Quanshu* (*Complete Library of the Four Treasures of Knowledge*) and the *Collected Works from the Past and Present*. The *Siku Quanshu* is now kept in Taiwan. The building itself is three-storied but has an appearance of a two-storied one. The Forbidden City used to have 9999.5 "rooms". The half "room" finds itself here at the western end of the building. In front of the building is a square pond spanned by three bridges.

Inner Cabinet

It was housed in a compound located at the southeastern corner of the Forbidden City, from across the Hall of Literary Glory. many officials served in the Inner Cabinet to help the emperor handle state affairs. They were Grand Scholars, Scholars, Reading Scholars, Readers, Filekeepers and Secretaries. They handled memorials and other documents presented to the emperor, drafted imperial decrees and other papers, kept imperial seals, placed documents on file, and handled translation work (Han, Manchu, Mongol and other languages).

Guard of Honor Regiment

Further to the east was the headquarters of the Guard of Honor Regiment. The size of the guard varied with different occasions. The biggest one, called "Dajia Lubu", for the ceremony at the Temple of Heaven, had 3,000 men. The one second to this, called "Fajia Lubu", for ceremony at the Gate of Supreme Harmony or the Meridian Gate, had 1,576 men. The other two had 200 men, called "Luanjia Lubu", and 300 men, called Qijia Lubu, for emperor's activities inside and outside the Imperial City respectively. "Lu" means shields and "bu" means books. They were so called because every such occasion was entered into books and a great number of the men held shields. The empress had a guard of honor of 77 men, a high consort had one of 36 to 58 men and a consort 28 men.

Imperial Stables and Falcon-Dog Yard

The stables were located behind the Pavilion of the Source of Literature. There used to be one stable for the emperor's riding horses, one for spare horses and one for Sichuan horses. Besides, there were kept 70 horses for ceremony use, 200 horses for draght purpose and 1,000 stock horses. As the emperors of the Qing dynasty were all crack riders, they were nicknamed "emperors on horseback". But the last three emperors were so weak in horsemanship that they were always helpt onto the horse when they took to riding.

The Qing sovereigns were very keen about dogs. They had sheds, clothings and so on specially made for their pet dogs. They also kept different kinds of rare birds and animals in the yard.

Imperial Viands Room (Kitchen)

During the Ming and Qing dynasties there were special terms refering to the emperor's eating: "consuming viands". The kitchen serving the emperor was called "Imperial Viands Room", and that serving the empress dowager called "Longevity Viands Room". There was a special kitchen preparing game food, such as deer meat, bear's paws, pheasant and wild goose.

An Inner Imperial Viands Room was located to the south of the Hall of Cultivating the Mind which served the emperor and his consorts, and an Outer Imperial Viands Room to the east of the Hall of Middle Harmony. But the Outer Viands Room was moved to the east of the Archery Pavilion in 1748 and the name was changed to Imperial Tea and Viands Room. The Longevity Viands Room was situated near the Palace of Motherly tranquility or the Palace of Tranquil Longevity, where the empress dowager's residence was situated. The Inner Viands Room was composed of the Meat Dish Bureau, Vegetarian Dish Bureau, Pastry Bureau, Rice Bureau and Roast Bureau.

The kitchen was staffed with well-known cooks recruited from various nationalities all over the country: Han, Manchu and Muslim. All the food was prepared strictly according to the menu. On the first of the tenth lunar month of 1747 Emperor Qian Long had for dinner fifteen dishes out of which four were prepared according to the recipe of the well-known cook Zhang Chengan. He did not find them as tasty as they should have been. So he ordered to have the cook Zheng himself do them again.

The kitchen had water carted from the Jade Spring and three different kinds of rice were grown arround Jade Spring Hill, Garden of Plenty and Hot Spring to provide for the palace. Ric was also supplied by the provinces as tribute.

The Imperial Tea and Viands Room was administered by the House-hold Department. An Administrative Minister, appointed by the emperor, supervised the dining of the royal family. Under him were:

Kitchen Controllers	3
Deputy Kitchen Controller	1
Tea Room Controllers	2
Deputy Tea Room Controller	1
Assistant Kitchen Controllers	12
Assistant Tea Room Controllers	6
Chief Cooks	4
Deputy Chief Cooks	4
Cooks	50
Chief "Bai-tang-e"	4
"Bai-tang-e"	41
Chief Waiters	5
Waiters	84
Chief Ushers	2
Ushers	11
Kitchen Odd Jobbers	28

Kitchen Odd Jobbers for Inner Imperial Viands Room   67

Daily provisions for the emperor were supplied by the Imperial Tea Viands Room: pork, 22 catties; pork for soup, 5 catties; lard, 1 catty; two lambs; five chickens; three ducks; cabbage, spinach, leek, coriander, 19 catties; etc. A hundred cows were kept for his milk consumption. Nine catties of tea leaves and 240 buns of steamed bread were supplied every day.

Imperial Hospital

It was staffed with a director, two deputy directors and a number of physicians of different ranks. The herbal medicine brew had to be prepared jointly by a physician who made the prescription, a eunuch and an official from the Household Department. The prescription would be sealed and signed by the physician and the eunuch and kept on file.

Before the emperor took the brew, it had to be taken by the physician, the deputy director and the eunuch to prove it poison-free. In case the imperial physician was not able to cure the emperor's illness, he would be punished.

Hall of Gathering Fragrance (Jiefangdian)

It was built in the reign of Emperor Qian Long as a new residence for the princes to replace the old one at the back of the Western Palaces. It has a green glazed-tile roof to signify youth. On the site of the hall before its construction there used to be an old courtyard where Emperor Tai Chang of the Ming dynasty had once lived when he was crown prince. In the fifth lunar month of 1615 an assassin was let in by two eunuchs. He broke into the courtyard with a wooden cudgel attempting on the life of the prince, but was subdued by the guards. The prince suspected that it was the plot of High Consort Zhen carried out by the two eunuchs. But he was afraid of her influence with the emperor. So, having the assassin and the two eunuchs put to death, he did nothing against the high consort.

Palace of Cultivating Happiness (Shuqinggong)

It is another residence for the princes built in 1679. It was originally meant for Crown Prince Yunreng. Later the emperor lived here with his brothers when he was crown prince. He moved out when he was seventeen. Emperor Jia Qing also lived here during his childhood from five until fifteen. He came back to this residence when he was enthroned and lived here for some time before moving to the Hall of Cultivating the Mind.

Hall for Ancestral Worship (Fengxiandian)

The Hall for Ancestral Worship is one of the nine imperial temples in Beijing. It was for worshipping ancestors of the emperor inside the palace. Another temple for this purpose was Taimiao (Imperial Ancestral Temple) outside the palace. The hall, located to the east of the Palace of Cultivating Happiness, was built in 1417 and renovated in 1656. It has a double-tiered hipped roof.

During the Qing dynasty the Hall of Ancestral Worship kept the memorial tablets of all the past emperors of the dynasty starting from the first one, Nuerhachi, down to the latest one. On either side were placed musical instruments. the rear hall kept memorial tablets of the four immediate ancesters of Nuerhachi.

On every New Year's Day, Winter Solstice, Longevity Day and other important festivals, the emperor came here to offer sacrifices to his ancestors. There were 26 such occasions out of a year. When the emperor came he would alight from the sedan-chair outside the courtyard and come in on foot to show his piousness. During major holidays 14 pairs of palace lanterns were hung besides 80 lamps were lit.

The emperor would practice abstinency the day before the sacrificial day. During the abstinence he would stay either at the Palace of Abstinence (for sacrifice at temples in the southern suburb) or at the East Warmth Chamber in front of the Hall of Cultivating the Mind (for sacrifice inside the Imperial City). In case the emperor was not able to perform the rite, a prince or high official would be dispatched on his behalf.

During the Ming dynasty offerings in

this hall were renewed every day. There were geese, bamboo shoots, plums, pears, oranges and sugar canes from the southern provinces transported to Beijing by boats on the Grand Canal. That involved a great manpower. In Nanjing alone boat pullers working for this task numbered over a thousand.

Archery Pavilion (Jianting)

It was built in the 7th lunar month of 1647, situated in an open ground to the south of the Hall of Ancestral Worship. The open ground was for the emperor and his sons and grandsons to practice shooting and equestrian skills. During a military service examination the emperor reviewed the martial arts of the candidates here.

The Qing Court built this pavilion in front of the Hall of Ancestral Worship to uphold the national tradition of the Manchus. Immediately after the Manchus took over the state power, they began to indulge in comfort and ease, and to learn the culture of the Han people, gradually giving up their hereditary militant spirit. Quite a number of Manchu noblemen found it greatly honored to be counted among scholars and men of letters at the cost of their military tradition. Afraid to lose this national spirit in the influence of the Han culture, Emperor Qian Long on many occasions, especially at an audience in 1752, warned against going back from Manchu customs and tradition. he had a

stone tablet erected to the east of the pavilion, bearing an inscription in his own handwriting to the same effect. A similar tablet was erected by Emperor Jia Qing in 1808 to the west of the pavilion.

Both of the emperors practiced shooting skills and martial arts on the range. Emperor Qian Long made shooting a subject of prime importance in military service examinations and constantly presided over it in person.

Hall of Martial Spirit (Wuyingdian)

At the beginning of the Ming dynasty it served as the residence of the emperor and was also used by the emperor to give audience to high officials. Later the residence moved to the Hall of Literary Glory. This place was used to house the court painters.

In 1466 the Ming dynasty was overthrown by Li Zicheng, a peasant rebellion leader. He used this hall as his office when he came into the palace on April 25th. Forty days later he was enthroned in this hall, but was forced by the invading Manchus to evacuate on the following day and died next year.

In the 19th year of Emperor Kang Xi's reign an editorial and printing office was established here at a house called Yudetang in the backyard. By an order of the emperor a great number of well-printed books with beautiful illustrations were published. Movable types of copper were used in the middle period of his reign. *The*

Collected Works from the Past and Present was compiled then, which took 25 years to complete. During the reign of his son Yong Zheng, it was revised and set to print. Only 64 volumes of this gigantic encyclopaedia, consisting of 10,000 juan, were brought out.

The year of the compilation of the greatest encyclopaedia in ancient times, *Siku Quanshu* (*Complete Library of the Four Treasures of Knowledge*) began in 1772 (37th year of the reign of Emperor Qian Long).

The job took ten years, with two famous scholars, Ji Yun and Lu Xixong as chief editors.

There is a well in the backyard and the printers drew water from it for use in their work.

Palace of Universal Peace (Xianangong)

It used to stand to the east of the Hall of Martial Spirit but was destroyed in a fire at the end of the Qing dynasty. On the wall surrounding the site were embeded four pieces of marble bearing inscriptions of four characters (meaning "upright and above board") in the handwriting of Emperor Kang Xi modeling on the original writing of Emperor Shun Zhi. The four characters on the horizontal board in the Palace of Heavenly Purity were a rubbing taken from the four stones here.

The side chambers had been the site of Tailoring Office responsible for the emperor's wear.

Hall of South Fragrance
(Nanxundian)

Situated to the south of the Hall of Martial Spirit the Hall of South Fragrance houses the portraits of emperors, empresses and officials of merit of various dynasties in the past.

Imperial Handwriting Office
(Yushufang)

Situated to the southwest of the Hall of Martial Spirit, it was the place where emperors' handwriting and specimen of calligraphy were carved.

Hall of Benevolence
and Wisdom
(Rezhidian)

In the Ming dynasty the coffins of the deceased emperors were placed here before burial. It was also the site of Imperial Institute of Painting where court painters served. Once the famous painter Daijing presented to the emperor a picture of his with a figure of a fisherman dressed in red. This incurred the displeasure of the emperor as the official in charge remarked that red was the color for officials not for a fisherman. So Daijing was dismissed for the offence.

In the Qing dynasty the head- quarters of the Household Department was established here. It administered the following offices to look after the domestic affairs of the emperor: the Storage Bureau, the Guard Bureau, the Protocol, the Accounting House, the Stock-Raising Bureau, the Disciplinary Bureau and the Construction Bureau. In addition, there were three offices governing the stables, the ordnance and gardens and farms.

The Office of Crafts
The Office of Cleaning
The Office of Heating
Ice Storage

All these were located behind the Household Department and were under the control of it. The different crafts consisted of picture mounting, box-making, carpentry, painting, seal-carving, lantern-making, shotgun, eye-glasses, glass ware, clocks, foundry, armor, ivory carving, bronzeware etc. The Office of Crafts was also responsible for interior furnishing. To celebrate the 60th birthday of Empress Dowager Ci Xi, the office spent 99,000 taels of silver for refurbishing all the horizontal boards and couplets in the palace. The daily cleaning of the palace involved a work force of two hundred.

The heating was tended by 25 eunuchs headed by two chief eunuchs. There were warm chambers in the living quarters of the royal family. Outside the window of a house there is a pit covered by wooden board. In winter a charcoal stove was put into the pit which would send heat through underground tunnels to the warm chamber inside. Daily charcoal supply varied: 120 catties for the empress dowager, 110 catties for the empress, 90 catties for a high consort, 75 catties for a consort, 30 catties for a princess and 20 catties for a prince.

The Ice Storage had five cellars to keep ice. Ice was taken from the moat in winter and kept in cellars for use in summer.

Inner Court— Residential Palaces of the Emperor and Empress

Behind the three great halls is a long open ground running from east to west, which serves as a demarcation line between the Outer Court and the Inner Court. Beyond Jingyunmen Gate at the east end of the ground are the Hall of Imperial Supremacy and the Palace of Tranquil Longevity for the retired emperor. Beyond Longzongmen Gate at the west end of the ground are the Palace of Motherly Tranquility and the Palace of Longevity and Health. Facing the Outer Court are three gates of the Inner Court: the Gate of Heavenly Purity in the middle, the Inner Right Gate to the west (leading to the Hall of Mental Cultivation of the Six Western Palaces), the Inner Left Gate to the east (leading to the Palace of Abstinence and the Six Eastern Palaces). Inside the Gate of Heavenly Purity, there are three rear palaces, namely the Palace of Heavenly Purity, the Hall of Union and the Palace of Earthly Tranquility. At the north end of the Inner Court is the Gate of Earthly Tranquility leading to the Imperial Garden.

The emperor lived in the Inner Court with his empress and scores of concubines, served by thousands of pa-lace maids. In the Ming dynasty, as many as 9,000 female attendants worked and lived in this palace at the same time. This fully illustrates the dissolute and debauched life of the Ming emperors.

The Gate of Heavenly Purity (Qianqingmen)

The Gate of Heavenly Purity, built like a mansion, is the main entrance to the Inner Court. It is decorated with golden dragon paintings and has three openings. Red gate slabs are placed in the back to make the porch look more spacious. On each side of the gate stands a glazed wall with floral patterns, which measures ten meters long and eight meters high. In front of the gate there are two gilded lions and some gilded water vats arranged in symmetry. All these, including bronze road lamps, make the Gate of Heavenly Purity more sumptuous and splendid.

Beginning from Emperor Kang Xi, the Qing emperors sometimes gave audience to government officials at this gate. It was one of the ways to show the emperor was dilligent at state affairs. When the official audience was given here, a throne would be placed in the middle of the Gate of Heavenly Purity. A desk with yellow covering was placed in front of the throne and a screen behind it. Before the desk, to the left, a felt mat was laid for the officials to kneel on. The body-guards stood on both sides of the throne. The guards with spears lined up on the terrace, and the guards with swords lined up below the marble ramp. All the officials stood in line according to their ranks to the east of the gate, facing the west. The court chroniclers, Hanlin and Kedao (all high officials) stood to the west of the gate, facing the east. The emperor was carried to the gate in a sedan-chair. As soon as the emperor seated himself, the court chronicler came up and stood near the western pillar, facing the east. A minister, a document box in hand, knelt down before the desk, put the box on it and then walked back, knelt down again and made a report to the emperor. After he finished, he retreated down the east steps. The other officials from different ministries also made reports in order of ranks. When this was over, a Manchu cabinet member held a file-box to the desk and knelt down. He then opened the box, took out the documents and began to report on various matters. The emperor gave his decree regarding each matter he reported. The cabinet members, in the mean time, took down all his decrees. Soon the audience came to and end. The emperor was carried back to his palace and all the officials took their leave. This ceremony was called "handing state affairs at the Imperial Gate". Among the Qing emperors, Kang Xi came here to give an audience most frequently, and some important decisions were made right in this place, such as the decision to quell down San Fan rebellion led by Wu San-gui. On the 4th day of the 10th lunar month of the 21st year of Kang Xi's reign, Shi Lang was dispatched to lead an expeditionary army to Taiwan. Next year they unified Taiwan and set up local governments there. In the 24th and 25th years of Kang Xi's reign it was decided at the Gate of Heavenly Purity that Marshal Peng Chung, Vice-Marshal Lang Tan and

Bandalsha, General Sabuso from Heilongjiang lead both the navy and the army to resist the Russian aggression. With the great assistance of the local people who fought bravely and heroically, they carried out two Yaksa campaigns and finally defeated the invading army. The Tsarist government was forced to agree to solve the border dispute through negotiations. In the 24th year of Kang Xi's reign, after the Qing army repelled the Tsarist aggression, Emperor Kang Xi, in order to show his determination to resist foreign aggression, made the decision at this gate to commend all the generals and soldiers for their meritorious deeds. All these decisions were of great historical significance in terms of the defense of national unity and territorial integrity.

Palace of Heavenly Purity (Qianqinggong)

The Palace of Heavenly Purity was built in the 18th year of Emperor Yong Le's reign in the Ming dynasty, and underwent renovations and repairs several times. The present structure dates back to the third year of Emperor Jia Qing's reign in the Qing dynasty. The double-eaved building rises 24 meters high and is decorated with minute paintings. It is the most important building in the Inner Court.

On the marble terrace of the palace, there are bronze tortoises, bronze cranes, a sundial and four gilded incense burners. Below the terrace on both sides of the main hall are two marble stands which are surmounted by two gilded tabernacles. The one on the east is called Jiangshan Hall and the one on the west Sheji Hall.

To the east of the main hall lies Sizhengxuan (the Room for Considering State Affairs) and to the west Yangdezhai (Studio for Cultivating Virtues). In the Qing dynasty, both east and west chambers had plaques with inscriptions by Emperor Qian Long. Kept in this palace were eight volumes of court records and battle charts used by Nuerhachi, the inperial seals of Emperor Kang Xi and Emperor Qian Long, stone rubbings, genealogical trees and the four treasures of the studio (writing brush, inkstick, paper and inkslab). In the east chamber there was a huge jade jar weighing 2,000 kilograms. It was 1.6 feet high, four feet long and three feet wide. The jade jar was carved in the palace workshop of the Qing dynasty during the period from the 41st year to the 44th year of Emperor Qian Long's reign.

In the centre of the main hall, there is a square platform with a throne and an ornate dragon screen, both of which are goldpainted and decorated with delicate carvings. The screen bears quotations from ancient Chinese classics, which were collected by Emperor Kang Xi. These quotations synthesized all the political trickery of the feudal rulers. Therefore they were carved on the screen to make them ever-lasting.

A couplet on the red pillars before the throne was written by Emperor Kang Xi and then copied by Emperor Qian Long. The meaning is that the emperor must cultivate his mind, be circumspect and farsighted before he could set an example for the whole nation; the emperor should disseminate widely the feudal ethics and never underestimate the difficulties in ruling over the people.

High up in the middle of the hall there is a plaque with an inscription which reads "Be open and above-board". The four characters were first written by Emperor Shun Zhi, then copied by Emperor Kang Xi. The present one dates from the 62nd year of Emperor Qian Long's reign.

The Palace of Heavenly Purity used to be the residence for emperors from the days of Emperor Yong Le in the Ming dynasty down to the reign of Emperor Shun Zhi and Emperor Kang Xi in the Qing dynasty. There are nine rooms in the east and west chambers altogether. Each room with three beds is divided into two stories. There are 27 beds in all, with staircases linking the upper floor and the lower floor. The empress sometimes stayed in this palace. The imperial concubines would be sent to the emperor's bedroom in proper order.

During the Ming dynasty the Palace of Heavenly Purity witnessed an assassination attempt that shocked the entire court and two unusual cases of treachery.

The aborted assassination took place on November 27, 1542. After mid-night when Emperor Jia Jing was fast asleep, a dozen court ladies worked together in an attempt to strangle him. One girl seized him by the throat and one girl stuffed his mouth with cloth. The other girls grabbed his four limbs, preventing him from moving. But unfortunately these girls were very young and acted in a panic. Instead of tying a running knot, they tied a Gordian knot. So they couldn't kill the emperor however hard they tried. After they were arrested, these palace-maids were all sentenced to death. Emperor Jia Jing was scared out of his senses and became very weak after the incident. It was seven or eight hours after the court doctor Xu Shen gave him the first aid treatment that the emperor regained his ability to speak. He was so frightened that even after his recovery he still did not dare to live in this palace again. He moved to the Palace of Imperial Longevity in the western part of the Forbidden City and lived there for more than 20 years. In the 45th year of his reign, the emperor was critically ill. He was moved back to the Palace of Heavenly Purity and died there on the same day.

Another incident the "Red Pills" happened in this palace 45 years later. On August 18, 1620, Emperor Wan Li died in the Hall of Immense Virtue in the west of the palace. On August 28, crown prince Zhu Changluo was enthroned. But he was seriously ill soon after coronation. He suffered from insomnia, lost his appetite and always felt dizzy. He found it difficult to walk and summoned two ministers, Fang Congzhe and Han Kuang, to his presence for a discussion about his funeral. During the session one official named Li Kezhuo presented the emperor with "Red Pills", which were claimed to be "elixir of life". Li Kezhuo took one pill first. The emperor also took one pill and felt much better after. On the afternoon of the same day,

the emperor took another pill presented by Li Kezhuo. But he died a sudden death at dawn the next day in the palace.

The third incident, known as the "Forced Relocation", followed in the wake of the case of "Red Pills" in the same year at the Palace of Heavenly Purity. After Emperor Tai Chang died, Li Xuanshi still hung on in the Palace of Heavenly Purity in an attempt to usurp the power in collaboration with her trusted eunuch Wei Zhongxian by taking advantage of the immaturity of the 16-year-old emperor. Li insisted she live together with the new emperor in the palace and be involved in handling state affairs. Some ministers, such as Liu Yijing, Zhou Jiamo, Yang Lian and Zuo Guangdou, objected strongly to Li's continued occupation of the emperor's residential palace, because they feared that she might turn the young emperor into a puppet and interfere with the state affairs. Liu Yijing, Han Kuang, Fang Congzhe and other ministers stood before the palace gate, demanding Li's relocation. Finally Li was forced to move from this palace to the Hall of Benevolence and Longevity in the east of the Forbidden City. In history this is called the case of "Forced Relocation".

On April 24, 1644, the peasant uprising troops led by Li Zicheng broke into the city of Beijing through Guang An Gate. Emperor Chong Zhen was in an impasse. He wrote a suicide note in the Palace of Heavenly Purity, ordered Empress Zhou to commit suicide in the Palace of Earthly Tranquility, wounded his 15-year-old princess Zhao Ren with his own sword and stabbed a number of

his concubines. After that he fled from the palace and hanged himself on Coal Hill. The next day at noon Li Zicheng entered the Imperial City through Xian City Gate and then occupied the Forbidden City. He destroyed the plaque with the inscription "Worship the Heaven and Respect the Ancestor", which was hung in the middle of the Palace of Heavenly Purity, and in its place he put up another plaque with the inscription "Worship the Heaven and Love the people". This showed the difference between the peasant power and the feudal empire.

During the reign of Shun Zhi and Kang Xi in the Qing dynasty, the Palace of Heavenly Purity still served as the emperor's residence. After his enthronement, Emperor Yong Zheng said that since his forfathers had resided in this palace for over sixty years, he did not have the heart to turn it into his own living quarters. So he decided to take up his residence in the Hall of Mental Cultivation. Nevertheless, he came to this palace to hold cabinet meetings with his ministers, give audience to government officials, read reports submitted by local officials, and receive foreign envoys. On such occasions as New Year's Day, Mid-Autumn Festival, winter solstice, New Year's Eve, the emperor's birthday, etc, the emperor would hold a grand ceremony or give a royal banquet in this palace.

In the Qing dynasty a royal family banquet was given in the palace on the eve of the Chinese New Year with the empress and concubines present. Another banquet was given on new Year's Day with the princes and princesses present.

The dinner table for the emperor was placed before the throne. The table for the empress was put to the east of the throne a little in the back. The tables for the concubines of different ranks stood on both sides of the throne. The close relatives of the emperor were also invited to the banquet. Usually two guests shared one table and the seating arrangements were strictly based on age. During the banquet, in order to add to the festival atmosphere, guests were sometimes asked to write poems on the spot.

In the 48th year of Qian Long's reign, a grand banquet was served in the palace to entertain imperial clansmen. The emperor invited all the princes, dukes, marquises, earls and other lower-ranking clansmen to the banquet, which was attended by 1,380 people in all. The emperor's brothers and marshals, 48 in number, dined in the main hall. The clansmen with official ranks or without dined on the marble terrace. The clansmen of distant relationship without official ranks dined on both sides of the central passageway, facing the north. Altogether 530 tables were set out for this magnificent banquet.

On the 15th of the 1st lunar month, a lantern banquet would be held in this palace to celebrate the Lantern Festival. It was called Full Moon Day, because people saw the full moon for the first time in the new year. It was customary for people to eat Yuanxiao (sweet dumplings) on that day. When night fell, all the colourful lanterns were lit and fireworks were set off. The people had a happy get-together and enjoyed the festivities. This custom dates back to 2,000 years ago.

In the Qing dynasty, Lantern Festival was celebrated mostly in the Imperial Garden. Sometimes a festival feast was held in the palace or outside Jingyun Gate to mark the occasion. Every year lanterns were hung everywhere in the Qing palace from December 24 to February 3. During the festival, 16 longevity lanterns and 128 lanterns of various sizes were dangling in front of the main palace building and nine huge lanterns under its eaves. Besides, five lanterns were hung at the Gate of Heavenly Purity, and one lantern was hung at the Gate of Sun Glory and the Gate of Moon Glory respectively. Below the marble terrace, a pagoda of lanterns was erected on each side of the courtyard. It had a 20-meter high wooden column entwined with dragons, on which over 1,000 lanterns in more than ten tiers were stacked up. Crickets caught in the last autumn were placed inside the lanterns so their chirping could be heard even in severe winter. During the night in the world of lanterns, the emperor, the empress and ministers had a wonderful time, drinking, eating sweet dumplings and enjoying the fascinating sight.

A grand banquet was also given in this palace for 1,000 elderly gentlemen. Throughout its history of 267 years, during the heyday under the rule of Kang Xi and Qian Long, the Qing court held such banquets four times. Fifty tables were set out in the verandas, 244 tables on the marble terrace, 124 tables on both sides of the central passageway, 382 tables on both sides of the marble terrace. They added up to 800 tables in all. The total number of guests invited to the banquet amounted to 3,000. After the banquet Manchu and Han officials composed as many as 3,429 poems praising the banquet. Qian Long granted each official one Ruyi (an S-shaped ornamental object) together with some silks and satins. The rest of the guests were bestowed one silver plaque each. The weight of the silver plaque varied with the age of the recipient: 10 taels for the 70-year-olds; 15 taels for the 75-year-olds; 20 taels for the 80-year-olds; 25 taels for the 85-year-olds; 30 taels for the 90-year-olds. In addition to these, 3,000 walking sticks and 4,822 purfume pouches were distributed among the guests.

This palace was also used to place the emperor's coffin. No matter where the emperor passed away, his coffin was always moved into the main hall here for the mourning service. In the early Qing dynasty the emperor gave audience to foreign envoys mostly in the Outer Court or in the imperial gardens. In the 59th year of his reign, Kang Xi received the Portuguese envoy in the Garden of Pleasant Spring. In the 58th year of his reign, Qian Long met with the British envoy at the Garden of Ten Thousand Trees inside the Royal Summer Resort in Rehe province. During the reign of Kang Xi and Qian Long, foreign envoys were sometimes received in the Palace of Heavenly Purity. In 1900 the Eight-Power Allied Forces occupied Beijing and signed the International Protocol of 1901 with the Qing court. From the 27th year to the 30th year of Guang Xu's reign, the ambassadors from the U.S., Britain, Germany, France, Portugal, Russia, Japan, Netherlands, Belgium, Austria and Italy, were all received in this palace. When an ambassador presented his credentials here, the Foreign Ministry would send a green palanquin with guards to the embassy. After the ambassador entered the palace, the guards would escort the palanquin to the Meridian Gate, where the ambassador would change to a sedan-chair. He then got off at Jingyun Gate and walked into the palace. The officials would show him to the imperial study for a short rest. At ten o'clock the emperor ascended the throne. After entering the main hall, the ambassador walked up the central steps, stood before the throne, and presented his credentials to the emperor. He then made his speech, which would be translated by an interpreter. When this was over, he would withdraw down the central steps, facing the emperor, who would then make a formal reply to the ambassador. The emperor's speech was first relayed by a prince and translated afterwards. The ambassador would bow to the emperor after his epeech and exit sideways from the left door, followed by the counsellor. He would take a short rest again in the imperial study, then walk out of the palace gate, get on the sedan-chair and ride through Jingyun Gate. He would then change to the original palanquin and return to the embassy by way of Donghua Gate.

A box containing the emperor's confidential appointment of his successor was kept behind a plaque with the inscription "Be open and above-board". In the Chinese history, most of the imperial rulers chose successors to the throne openly. The appointment of the crown prince was made public long time in advance, so as to prepare him for the succession. The crown prince was either the emperor's eldest son or one of his sons. In case the emperor didn't have any son, his brother could succeed to the crown. This age-old practice had been followed from Yin and Zhou dynasties down to Ming and Qing dynasties.

Since he was enthroned, Yong Zheng had learned a good lesson from his predecessor in the matter of appointing the crown prince. He himself saw the reqeated appointment and repeated deposal during the reign of Kang Xi, and he experienced the bitter struggle among the princes for the throne. In view of the disadvantages in open appointment of the crown prince, Yong Zheng began to adopt confidential appointment of his successor. The box containing the emperor's appointment was hidden behind a plaque with the inscription "Be open and above-board". This meant the emperor would not make public who was the crown prince when he was still alive. After the emperor died, the ministers would open the box together and declare the successor to the throne. In case of contingency, another copy of the decree on the appointment was made secretly and kept in the Royal Secretariat. On October 7, 1735, Yong Zheng died. Prince Zhuang, Prince Guo, Minister Ertai and Zhang Tingyu jointly opened the sealed box and took out the imperial decree. They declared Hong Li, the fourth son, the successor to the throne, who became the fourth emperor of the Qing dynasty with the reign title Qian Long.

In the 38th year of Qian Long's reign, the confidential imperial decree hidden in the box declared the 15th son the successor to the throne, who then became the 5th emperor of the Qing dynasty. On the 10th day of the 4th lunar month of the 4th year of his reign, Emperor Jia Qing wrote a decree, appointing his second son Min Ning, the crown prince and put it in the box. On the 25th day of the 7th lunar month of the 25th year of his reign, Jia Qing was critically ill. He summoned the ministers to his presence and asked them to open the box and declare Min Ning the crown prince, who then became the 6th emperor of the Qing dynasty with the reign title Dao Guang. Emperor Dao Guang considered both Yi Zhu, the fourth son, and Yi Zin, the sixth son, were eligible to become the crown prince. Yi Zhu was borne by the empress, but Yi Xin bore a strong resemblance to the emperor in appearance and nature. Therefore Dao Guang hesitated to decide between Yi Zhu or Yi Xin as the crown prince. Then he had a plan to test and judge the two sons. It happened to be the time for spring hunting at Nanyuan. He ordered all the princes to go with him. Yi Xin made the best bag. But Yi Zhu, who had taken the hint from Du Shoutien, didn't shoot even one arrow. When the emperor asked why, he answered, "Now spring has come. It is the mating season, so I couldn't have the heart to hurt these animals." Dao Guang was quite pleased with his reply and said, "That's exactly what an emperor should have said." Hence the decision on the appointment was made. On August 7, 1846,

Dao Guang wrote the imperial decree on the appointment in both Manchu and Han languages, which read, "The 4th son Yi Zhu is appointed the crown prince and the 6th son Yi Xin is granted the title Senior Prince." This imperial decree on the appointment of the crown prince is the only one preserved to this day. The decrees for this purpose during the reign of Yong Zheng, Qian Long and Jia Qing were all lost. Such confidential appointment of the crown prince had, in certain period, mitigated the struggle for power within the royal family, and straightened out the past confused situation in terms of the succession to the crown.

Zhao Ren Hall

To the east of the Palace of Heavenly Purity lies the Zhao Ren Hall. It was earlier called the Hong De Hall and renamed the Zhao Ren Hall in 1583, because it was the residence of Princess Zhao Ren, a daughter of Emperor Chong Zhen of the Ming dynasty. In the 9th year of Qian Long's reign in the Qing dynasty, all the rare books kept in the Imperial Palace since the Ming dynasty were all put together in this hall. These books were printed respectively in the Song, Jin, Yuan and Ming dynasties. The plaque hung high in the middle of the hall was inscribed with Qian Long's handwriting "Tian Lu Lin Lang" (A superb collection of books), which was based on the story about the Tianluge Pavilion, an imperial library in the Han dynasty.

Hall of Great Virtue (Hongdedian)

To the west of the Hall of Heavenly Purity lies the Hall of Great Virtue. In the Ming dynasty, Emperor Wan Li sometimes conferred with the ministers here. On August 18, 1620, Wan Li died in this hall.

In the Qing dynasty, Shun Zhi, Kang Xi and Guang Xu summoned officials from various ministries here and listened to their reports. Emperor Tong Zhi once used this hall as his classroom, and hired two teachers, Li Hongzao, an academician, and Wong Tongsu, the No. 1 of the national civil examination. In the 4th year of his reign, Tong Zhi granted Wong Tongsu free access to the Hall of Great Virtue.

A tea house in the eastern section was located in the first room to the left of the Gate of Heavenly Purity. The water for brewing the tea was carried here from Jade Spring Hill in the western suburbs. Next to it was the Imperial Study, where the sons and grandsons of the emperor had their lessons.

South of the Gate of Sun Glory was the Royal Pharmacy. The two plaques hung in this chamber had inscriptions in Kang Xi's handwriting, which read "Pharmacy" and "Long- evity" respectively. The pharmacy had a constant supply of medicine to meet the needs of the emperor, the empress and the imperial concubines. Altogether there were more than

400 kinds of medicine stored here. When they went to see their patients in different palaces, the imperial physicians were always escorted by eunuchs of the Royal Pharmacy.

North of the Gate of Sun Glory was the storehouse where chiming clocks were kept. Beyond the Clock Storehouse was the Duanning Hall, in which there was another plaque with an inscription in Kang Xi's handwriting. This three-room hall was used to store the emperor's crown, robes, belts and shoes. The inkslabs and inksticks used by Kang Xi, Yong Zheng and Qian Long were kept here, too.

Further north was the Imperial Teahouse. Its name on the plaque was written by Kang Xi. This teahouse provided tea only for the emperor. The empress and the empress dowager had their seperate teahouses. The water for brewing the tea was carried here from Jade Spring Hill by special carts everyday. All these carts were flying dragon flags, so that they could pass freely anywhere. Jade spring Hill is located 15 kilometers to the northwest of Wanpin county in the west of Beijing. There is a stone cave in the south of the the hill. Two Chinese characters meaning "Jade Spring" were engraved in the stone above the cave. The spring comes out of a stone crack and a gargoyle was carved out of that stone. Because the spring water was sweet and refreshing, Emperor Qian Long named it "the No. 1 Spring in China", and wrote "the bubbling Jade Spring", which was later carved on the surface of a stone tablet.

In the western part close to the Gate of Heavenly Purity was the guard-house with ten guards and one official on duty. To the west was Jingshifang, the Administrative Office in charge of court eunuchs.

West of Jingshifang was the South Study. It began to exist in 1677, when Kang Xi ordered Academician Zheng Ying and Minister Gao Shiqi to come on duty in this room. In 1694 four officials from the Imperial Academy and the Imperial College began to be on duty here in turn everyday. It was in this study that Kang Xi arrested the powerful minister Aobai by resourcefulness. Kang Xi was put on the throne as the second emperor of the Qing dynasty at the age of eight, when his father Shun Zhi died. Shortly before his death, Shun Zhi issued a decree, appointing Suoni, Sukesaha, Ebilong and Aobai as regents to assist the young emperor in governing the country. Suoni was advanced in years and in poor health. Ebilong was mentally weak and afraid to do anything unconventional. Sukesaha was not as powerful as the other regents. Therefore, of the four regents, Aobai was the most powerful and the most influential. He formed his own clique to pursue selfish interests, and usurped the power to exercise dictatorship. Most of the high ranking officials were either his family members or his relatives. He made important decisions at his home and executed them directly, making a puppet of the emperor. Kang Xi formally took over the reins of the government on August 25, 1667, when he reached the age of 14. On the lunar New Year's Day in the 8th year of Kang Xi's reign, Aobai led the ministers into the palace to extend new year

greetings to the emperor. He was dressed in a yellow robe with a red velvet tie on his hat just like an emperor. Sometimes he pretended to be sick and refused to go to court. When Kang Xi went to his residence to see him, Aobai even laid a knife on his bed. He should have been punished for attempted assasination, but Kang Xi said, "It is the Manchu custom to bear arms at all times. What's there to be alarmed at?" Even so, Kang Xi was still very much worried about Aobai's imperious and despotic behavior. Since Aobai's clique was a great threat to his power, Kang Xi decided to get rid of him by some subtle ruse. First he summoned Suotu, the son of Suoni, to the palace for secret planning under pretence of playing chess with him. He also chose some young boys from among the army officers' families and brought them into the palace, where they practised wrestling and fist-fighting under pretence of playing games with the emperor. Aobai thought Kang Xi had no ambition at all and deemed it easy to make a fool of the young emperor. Kang Xi, in order to slacken his vigilance, showed more courtesy to him. This made Aobai even more arrogant and presumptuous. Naturally Kang Xi did not resign himself to being a puppet emperor, and was determined to do away with him. On June 14, 1669, the 16-year-old emperor summoned Aobai to the South Study. Everything went according to plan. After Aobai entered the study, a servant offered him a chair with a broken leg, and served him tea in a cup which had just been brought outof boiling water. The cup burnt Aobai's hand and fell on the floor

in pieces. The servant behind Aobai's chair wasted no time, pushing the chair forward and throwing him on the floor. Kang Xi immediately called out, "How impolite Aobai is!" No sooner had he finished than came out a dozen guards and the young wrestlers. Aobai was arrested on the spot and sentenced to life imprisonment on 30 counts. Kang Xi eliminated Aobai by wisdom and seized back the political power. This opened the way for rapid social development in the early Qing dynasty.

South of the Gate of Moon Glory was the Inner Fileroom, where 34 eunuchs worked with one eunuch of the eighth official rank in charge. Everyday the officials from the Outer Fileroom handed in the memorials and petitions submitted by high officials to the Inner Fileroom. The eunuchs on duty here would then present the memorials or petitions to the emperor. After the emperor read these documents and wrote his comments on them, they would be returned to the Inner Fileroom and subsequently sent back.

North of the Inner Fileroom was the office in charge of the emperor's sedan-chairs and palanquins. There were 32 eunuchs working here under the supervision of two chief eunuchs. Their duties involved assigning work to the sedan carriers, and arranging teams of retainers for night shifts at the emperor's residence.

Further north from the Gate of Moon Glory was the Cabinet Fileroom. Everyday official papers from the Cabinet were delivered to the officials here, who then presented them to the emperor for comments or approval. After they were looked through and signed by the emperor, these documents would be returned to this office. The officials here put down short notes in red ink on the cover of the documents, before sending them back. In this office seven people were engaged in clerical work under one supervisor.

The Hall of Diligence was located north of the Cabinet Fileroom. In the Qing dynasty, the four Treasures of the Studio—writing brushes, inksticks, paper and inkslabs, together with classical works, were stored here, after they were viewed or used by the emperor. Three days after the final imperial ex- amination, emperor Yong Zheng came here to review the test papers of the successful candidates from No. 1 to No. 10. during the reform movement of 1898, emperor Guang Xu gave banquets here to entertain ministers and held discussions with them on political affairs.

The Hall of Diligence had a rear hall closely behind it, where Kang Xi used to have his private lessons when he was the crown prince. In autumn every year, the Cabinet and the Privy Council held a joint meeting, after which they met with the emperor in this hall and reported to him the decisions on some important criminal cases sent in by the Ministry of Justice. The emperor would look carefully through the list of the condemned and marked down those to be executed with red ink. This was termed "Autumn Sentence" in history.

The Hall of Union
(Jiaotaidian)

Behind the Hall of Heavenly Purity is the Hall of Union, which is square in shape with an impressive spire.

The name of the hall was based on a quotation from one of the oldest Chinese classics —"Heaven and earth are united". The Hall of Union is located between the Hall of Heavenly Purity and the Hall of Earthly Tranquility, symbolizing the intercourse of Heaven and Earth, and also the harmonious relationship between the emperor and the empress. On lunar New Year's Day and the empress's birthday, the empress ascended the throne in this hall, as imperial concu-bines and the high officials' wives filed in to extend their greetings to her. After that, all the princes came in to make obeisance to the empress, who then bestowed money on them in return. All together nine taels of gold and 900 taels of silver were given away as grants on such occasions. According to historical records, early emperors personally did some farm work and the empresses personally bred silkworms. The Qing emperors and empresses also followed this ancient practice. In the third lunar month the empress went to the Silkworm Altar, where she held a ceremony to start silkworm breeding that year. As a rule the empress kept a fast of two days before the ceremony. The day before the Silkworm Day, baskets and sickles were brought to the Hall of Union for a

preview by the empress. On the Silkworm Day, the royal procession with guards of honour flying flags were waiting outside Shunzhen Gate. Presently the empress carried in a palanquin left the Forbidden City through the North Gate (the Gate of Divine Prowess), followed by imperial concubines, princesses and officials' wives. A total of 5,000 armed guards lined up along the way from the North Gate to the Silkworm Altar. Another 5,000 guards were deployed around the altar. Having taken a short rest by the altar, the empress went to the mulberry garden, where she, with a gold sickle, cut one branch off the first mulberry tree in the east, then moved on to the first tree in the west and cut off two branches. Afterwards she took her seat on the reviewing stand, watching the concubines and the officials' wives cut off mulberry branches. Kneeling down on the ground, the silkworm breeders took over the mulberry leaves picked by the empress and the imperial concubines, and then spread them over the silkworms. Before the ceremony came to an end, the concubines and other ladies had to bow six times, kneel down three times and kowtow three times to the empress to conclude this silkworm-breeding ceremony.

When silkcocoons were ready for collecting, the empress led all the imperial concubines to the silkworm-breeding room and do symbolic reeling personally. The silk thus obtained was dyed red, green, black and yellow and used for making the emperor's ceremonial robes worn at sacrificial rites.

Twenty-five imperial seals of the

Qing emperors are kept in the Hall of U-nion. They were used for different government documents, as stipulated under the reign of Emperor Qian Long. They are made of gold, jade or sandal-wood. The jade seals are made of white jade, sapphire or jasper. The handles of these seals are in the shape of drapons in various postures. The size of the seals ranges from 2.1 inches square to six inches spuare. In the early days 39 seals were stored in the Hall of Union. In 1746, Qian Long decided to keep 25 seals in this hall. The rest of them were stored away in the Phoenix Tower of the old Qing Palace in Shengjing (present-day Shenyang) in Northeast China.

It was in accordance with the Heavenly Number that the emperor chose 25 seals and not more. According to the ancient classics, 25 is the Heavenly Number, because the odd numbers 1, 3, 5, 7, 9, of the ten digits add up to 25. Qian Long understood that no dynasty in history had ever had a perpetual life, and it was difficult to predict how long the Qing dynasty would last. He hoped that, by keeping 25 seals, the Qing dynasty could rule the country continuously for at least 25 generations. He would have been quite satisfied if, with blessings from heaven, his wish would come true, for he knew quite well that not one dynasty in the Chinese history had ever managed to maintain its rule until the 25th generation. Nevertheless, his prayers did not work. The Qing dynasty was overthrown on the 10th generation.

The 25 seals are all carved in Manchu and Han languages except one.

The imperial seals symbolized the power of the emperor and were regarded as the proof of official authority. The 25 imperial seals were listed below together with their respective functions.

1. The Seal of Divine Mandate. It symbolized the end of the Ming dynasty and the beginning of the Qing dynasty by the grace of God.

2. The Seal of Obediance. It symbolized the obediance of the Qing emperor to the order of heaven in his rule of the country.

3. The Seal of Heavenly Norms. It was used to imply that the Qing court acted according to the heavenly norms.

4. The Seal of Emperor (in Manchu). It was used on the imperial decrees dealing with such matters as the emperor's coronation, crown succession and the final imperial examination.

The Four seals were used during the reign of the first four emperors— Huangtaiji, Shun Zhi, Kang Xi and Yong Zheng.

5. The Seal of Emperor (made of sandalwood). It was used for such documents as crowning of the empress or proclamation of grand ceremonies.

6. The Seal of Heavenly Son. It was used for funeral orations or elegiac address at sacrificial rites.

7. The Seal of Imperial Titles. It was used for the edicts announcing the titles of praise conferred on the emperor or the empress.

8. The Seal of Kinship. It was used when the emperor gave promotion or honourable titles to his clan relatives.

9. The Seal of Commendation. It was used when the emperor bestowed yellow gown and jacket or Ruyi on officials with meritorious deeds.

10. The Seal for Army Recruitment.

11. The Seal for granting official titles to the nobility of minority nationalities.

12. The Seal for the imperial decrees issued to minority areas or vassal states.

13. The Seal for officual documents admonishing officials to work hard in consolidating the feudal rule.

14. The Seal for royal edicts issued to officials above the fifth rank.

15. The Seal for royal edicts issued to officials under the sixth rank.

16. The Seal for royal edicts glorifying the strength of the country or making the merits and virtues of the emperor known to everybody throughout the country.

17. The Seal for royal edicts commending military officials or granting official promotion.

18. The Seal for official documents concerning cultural and educational affairs.

19. The Seal for royal edicts to publicize ancient classic works which were beneficial to the consolidation of feudal rule.

20. The Seal used by the emperor on inspection tours outside the capital.

21. The Seal for dispatching armed forces to suppress peasant uprisings or sending a punitive expedition against minority groups.

22. The Seal used by the emperor when issuing orders to the royal army.

23. The Seal used for letters to foreign

envoys or for written replies to minority governments.

24. The Seal for imperial decrees issued to the whole country.

25. The Seal for plaques with inscriptions in the emperor's own hand-writing.

The first four seals had been handed down from the early days of the Qing dynasty prior to its conquest of the entire country. The other 21 seals were used regularly for court affairs in later days. The Cabinet was in charge of all these seals, and the eunuch chief was responsible for keeping them in good condition. However, the Cabinet must ask the emperor for permission before they took out the seal from the box and made its impression on official documents.

There was a chiming clock in this hall. It was made in 1798 by the Works Department of the Imperial Board. The clock is set in a wooden case with delicate carvings and golden drawings in an antiquated and simple style. It is 564.8 cm high in three tiers, and sits on a stand 220.8 cm by 176.15 cm. The facade of the second tier is the dial plate of the clock, which is 96cm in diameter with an hour and a minute hand. The 12 figures on the dial are Roman numerals. Behind the clock is an 8-step staircase, 268.8 cm in hight, up which the attendants may get to the second tier to wind up the clock. There are three copper gearings, of which the middle one is connected with the two hands, the left one controls the striking of hours, and the right one controls the striking of quarters. A large piece of lead is linked to each gearing by a leather strap as the movement weight or the

striking weight (over 50 kilograms). Everyday the attendant pulled up the lead weights so that they would come down at the fixed speed, thereby turning the gearings to rotate, and the clock would tick away continuously. The chiming was sonorous and could reach every corner of the Inner Court.

On the east side of the hall stands a clepsydra (water clock), a time-piece used in ancient China. It was believed in the ancient times that the Yellow Emperor invented the clepsydra. Throughout the Chinese history every dynasty had officials specially assigned the job of taking care of the clepsydra in the imperial court. The one kept in this hall is still in perfact condition and regarded as a treasure. According to the inscription on it, this water clock was made in 1746.

The clepsydra is set in a wooden pavilion, about five meters in height. It is composed of five bronze vessels. Each vessel has a small hole at the bottom. When the uppermost vessel is filled with water, it begins to drip evenly through the holes. There is a figurine on top of the lowest container. The calibrated scale in his hands floats with the rising water and time is indicated on the markings. At 12 o'clock noontime everyday, two eunuchs would discharge the water in the lowest container and fill up the highest container to start the dripping again.

Palace of Earthly Tranquility (**Kunninggong**)

To match the Palace of Heavenly Purity, this palace was named the Palace of Earthly Tranquility, so that the two palaces representing heaven and earth respectively would symbolize the eternity of feudal rule. this palace was first built in the 18th year of Yong Le's reign in the Ming dynasty and was rebuilt in the 12th year of Shun Zhi's reign in the Qing dynasty, after the fashion of the Palace of Purity and Tranquility in Shengjing (Shenyang today). It is double-eaved and decorated with minute paintings of dragons and phoenixes. Inside the hall, along the gable there is a long platform. A bow and a quiver used to be hung from the pillar beside it. There are some lattice windows both in front and in the back with paper pasted on the outside, which was the Manchu custom in those days. The gate of the palace used to be in the middle of the building, but it was moved to the east wing in the Qing dynasty.

The palace is nine-bay wide. The Western Warm Chamber, with windows but no doors, was the place for the altar. The space of four bays in the middle was used to offer sacrifices to the gods. The space of two bays in the east wing, known as the Eastern Warm Chamber, was the imperial bridal chamber.

The Palace of Earthly Tranquility was the residence of the empress during the Ming and Qing times. In 1644, when the peasant uprising leader Li Zicheng seized Beijing, Empress Zhou of Emperor Chong Zhen committed suicide here. In the Qing dynasty, after Yong Zheng moved his residence to the Hall of Mental Cultivation, the Palace of Earthly Tranquility became the empress's residence only in name. The empress usually chose one of the six palaces on either side of the Inner Court as her residence. For example, Qian Long's empress lived in the Palace of Eternal Spring, Tong Zhi's empress lived in the Palace of Gathering Elegance, Guang Xu's empress lived in the Palace of Quintessence.

The Eastern Warm Chamber of the palace now still looks the same as it was when Emperor Guang Xu was married here. When entering the chamber through the main entrance of the palace, one first sees a red wooden screen wall. At its center is a large sign of double-happiness covered with gold leaf, and in its four corners are patterns of a dragon and a phoenix embracing each other, symbolizing the happy marriage of the emperor and empress. In-side, close to the northern wall is a couch sheltered by a wooden structure with intricate carvings and a shrine was on its ceiling above the couch. To the west is the bridal bed also sheltered by a wooden structure with carved open-work. The mattress has red satin covering embroidered with the pattern of double happiness. At each end of the bridal bed is a small side table made of red sandal wood and carved with motif of dragons and phoenixes. A pair of "Happiness" lanterns is set on each of the side table. In the center of the bed stands a gold vase, containing jewelery, gold, silver and grain, hence the name "a hundred treasure vase". A drapery over the entire bed is made of red satin and embroidered with the design of dragons, phoenixes and a hundred young boys in various postures, symbolizing the fertility of the imperial family. Over the front of the bed is hung a plaque with an inscription, which reads "The sun at dawn and the moon at the first quarter", referring to the emperor and the empress. On the back wall behind the couch is an imperial motto, which is a copy of Qian Long's calligraphy, made in the 4th year of Xian Feng's reign. On the left side of the couch there is a side table with a porcelain vase and a hatstand on it. On the right there is another side table with some classical books on it.

By the south window there is a long brickbed covered with two red satin mattresses with an embroidered pattern of double happiness. An amber phoenix stands on the table at the center of the bed. This was where the emperor and empress drank the nuptial wine and enjoyed the wedding dinner. All the walls in the bridal chamber are red in colour. On the floor there used to be a colourful carpet with the design of dragons, phoenixes and double happiness. A big palace lantern is suspended from the ceiling, shedding red light everywhere and suffusing the room with a pleasant atmosphere.

Only those emperors who were not married at the time of succession to the throne had their wedding ceremony in the Palace of Earthly Tranquility. Since its conquest of the whole country, the Qing dynasty had ten emperors in power, of whom five emperors (Yong Zheng, Qian Long, Jia Qing, Dao Guang and Xian Feng) ascended the throne after they were married. Therefore their consorts became the empresses in the wake of the succession. Naturally there were no wedding ceremony in this case. Four emperors (Shun Zhi, Kang Xi, Tong Zhi and Guang Xu) were married after they were enthroned. According to historical records, Kang Xi, Tong Zhi and Guang Xu held their wedding ceremonies in the Palace of Earthly Tranquility. The last emperor Pu Yi also was married in this palace after his abdication. These emperors were still in their teens at the time of marriage. When Shun Zhi was 14-years old, his mother Empress Dowager Xiaozhuangwei, prompted by Regent Duoergun, chose the daughter of Prince Wu Keshan as the future empress. They got married on the 13th day of the 8th lunar month in the 8th year of Shun Zhi's reign. Kang Xi chose the granddaughter of Regent Suoni as the future empress at the age of 12, and got married on the 8th day of the 9th lunar month in the 4th year of his reign. Tong Zhi, at the age of 17, chose the daughter of Academician Cong Yi as the future empress and got married on the 15th day of the 9th lunar month in the 11th year of his reign. Guang Xu, at the age of 18, married his cousin who was chosen for him by Empress Dowager Ci Xi. The last emperor Pu Yi, at the age of 17, chose his consort by himself and got married on December 1, 1922.

In the Qing dynasty sacrifices were

offered to the gods in the ritual hall of the Palace of Earthly Tranquility everyday except the days of fast and the days when killing animals was prohibited. According to Manchu custom, the sacrificial rites had to be held in the formal residence. The Qing rulers carried on this old practice, which dated back to the Jin dynasty. For the more important sacrificial rites either in spring or in autumn, 39 pigs were butchered as offerings to the gods. (Only pigs without defects were selected as sacrifice.) After the pig was killed, its blood was put in a silver basin. Its ear tip, gall, bladder, trotters and tail were placed in a plate, which was put on the left side of the altar together with the blood basin. This ritual dated back to ancient times. A long U-shaped platform lies along the southern, western and northern walls of the main hall. Gods' tablets for morning service were arranged on the platform to the west and those for afternoon service to the north. On the western wall a Korean-style bag (popularly known as offspring bag 2.1 feet long and 1.4 feet wide) kept used necklaces with lock-shaped pendants worn by babies.

In the middle of the hall are two small black tables with bells, a tambourine, a Chinese lute, a 3-stringed guitar, a kettle drum, castanets, swords and arrows on top. A couch for the emperor is set on the platform to the south. Another couch for the empress dowager is set on the platform to the north. There is a lamp on each side of the couch. In the east of the hall is a kitchen with three cauldrons in it, two of which were used to cook meat and one used for steaming cakes.

The iron hooks and slices used for cooking the meat are hung on the window lattice and an iron lamp sits on the windowsill. There is a niche in the east wall with the tablet for the Kitchen God. On the 23rd day of the 12th lunar month every year, the emperor came here, bowed three times to the tablet, and then prayed to Heaven and Earth for happiness in the new year.

Besides daily service, monthly and seasonal sacrificial rites were also performed in this palace. The most important ones took place in the 2rd and 8th lunar months and on the 2rd day of the new year, when the emperor, empress and the empress dowager all came to the flagpole in front of the palace to worship the gods. Princes, dukes, marquises and ministers were also present at the rite. The offerings included two white horses, two oxen, two gold ingots weighing five taels each, two silver ingots weighing 50 taels each, 10 bolts of silk and 40 bolts of cloth. After the service the emperor sat down in the couch to the south and the empress dowager to the north. Princes and the ministers were seated on the floor facing the west. Then wine, meat, soup and rice were served. The diners cut the meat with their own knives and must not lay down the bowls and spoons until the emperor finished his meal.

The meat left over was distributed among the superintendent and the guards. At daybreak every morning, the eunuchs on duty would call out, "Please have meat, gentlemen." Hearing the call, the guards at the Gate of Heavenly Purity, the physician on duty at the royal clinic

and the adjucts of the emperor all came to the Palace of Earthly Tranquility. Each of them brought a felt mat to sit on below the south window, and was served a large piece of sacrificial meat with some salt. When they finished eating, they held up their plates and eunuchs came and take them away. In case the portion was not enough, they could ask for more. Every year 700 piculs of glutinous sorghum was consumed to make cakes and wine, and more than 1,300 pigs were butchered for the sacrificial rites held at this palace. The General Service Department spent 22,000 taels of silver on raising pigs to meet this need.

Behind the palace is the Gate of Earthly Tranquility. The rooms on both sides of the gate were used by the eunuchs on duty. West of the Studio of Repose was the room for the royal physician on duty. Beyond the gate is the Imperial Garden, which was called "Back Garden" in the Ming times. On each side of the gate stands a catalpa surrounded by a ring of bricks. It is said that in fighting for the unification of China and consolidation of the border areas, whenever the Qing emperor won a victory, a lump of soil was brought to the palace and laid around the catalpa, symbolizing the conquest of new land.

Imperial Garden

The Imperial Garden, the oldest garden in the Forbidden City, occupies an area of more than 12,000 square meters. Centering around the Hall of Imperial

Peace, the garden has over 10 pavilions, terraces and towers laid out in symmetry and is beautifully embellished with fantastic rockeries, ancient cypress trees, bamboo groves and exotic flowering plants.

The Hall of Imperial Peace was built in the Ming times with a flat roof, which was very rare among ancient buildings. It was originally surrounded by bamboo groves. In 1535 a brick wall was added around it when it was under reconstruction. The main entrance was first called "Tianyizhimen", and re-named "Tianyimen" (The only entrance to heaven) in the Qing dynasty. Inside the hall stands the statue of the King of Xuan Wu flanked by bronze statues. On the right is a bronze bell and on the left is a gold-painted drum. Taoist mass was held in the 1st, 2nd, 5th, 8th, 9th, 10th and 11th lunar months. On lunar New Year's Day the emperor came here to worship the King of Xuan Wu, who was believed to be the Water God and could, therefore, prevent the palace buildings from catching fire.

In front of the hall, on the left are the Fragrance Pavilion and a glazed furnace; on the right is a marble base, about two meters high, carved with a motif of dragons. The marble base was used for an army flagpole which was also carved with nine dragons entwining it. To the west of the marble base is the Army Flag God's Temple.

In front of the Tianyimen Gate are two gilt "Xie Zhi", a mythical animal. Twelve rocks of grotesque shape stand on two sides of the gate, symbolizing 12

months. Farther to the left is a large piece of quartzite, resembling sea cucumbers. On the right is "Zhuge Liang Worshipping the Big Dipper" Rock. A strangely shaped rock embedded in a carved marble foundation, known for its natural design: an old man in a silk headdress and a purple long-sleeved gown, bowing with both hands clasped in front seeming to worship the stars in the sky.

East of the Hall of Imperial Peace lies the Hill of Collecting Excellence. The Hall of Looking at Flowers used to be located here in the early Ming period. On April 17, 1583 the hall was dismantled and an artificial hill was built with rocks in its place. In the Qing times, a horizontal board over the gateway had an inscription in both Manchu and Han languages, which read "Collecting Excellence". On the left of the gateway there is a foot-stone with two engraved Chinese characters "Cloud Root" in Qian Long's handwriting. Behind the gateway are stone steps leading to the Pavilion of Imperial Landscape on top of the hill. Every year on the Double Ninth Festival (the 9th day of the 9th lunar month) the emperor, empress and imperial concubines came here to ascend this height and enjoy a feast of the scenic beauty both within and outside the Forbidden City.

Before the hill there is a fountain on each side, which has a stone base in the shape of a lion and a spout in the shape of a mythical animal.

Beside the hill stands a 400-year-old cypress, which was called "The Sunshading Marquis Tree". Legend says that the old cypress withered when Emperor Qian

Long went south of the Yangtze River on an inspection tour. It was a hot summer, but the emperor felt, however, that he was always shaded by a tree. The cypress revived after the emperor returned to the capital, so Qian Long believed the cypress must be a divine tree, and was pleased he could get its protection. The emperor conferred on it the title "Sunshading Marquis" and wrote a poem about it. A gardener was specially assigned to look after this cypress and received the salary of a marquis.

Next to the old cypress is Li Zao Hall. It was built under the reign of Qian Long to house the well-known encyclopedia *The esentials of Si Ku Quan Shu*, a famous collection of Chinese ancient books.

Its compilation was begun in 1772. At that time Qian Long was already 63 years old and he was afraid that he would not be able to see the completion of compiling such vol-uminous work, so he ordered that the best parts be put into "the essentials", which was completed in the 43rd year of his reign. It had 12,000 volumes, but only two copies were made by hand of each volume. One complete set was kept in Li Zao Hall (now in Taiwan), and the other was kept in Yuanmingyuan Garden, but it was destroyed by the Anglo-French invading army in 1860. This hall, shaded by old trees, is situated in a quiet corner with pavilions in front and an artificial hill to its right.

To the southeast of the Hall of Imperial Peace is the House of Crimson Snow, which was built during the reign of Qian Long. The lattice work of the windows is characterized by four Chinese characters meaning "Longevity". The beams and columns were painted green to look like bamboo, and therefore noted for the simple and unique style. In front of it are some crabapple trees which bear white and crimson flowers, hence the name of the house.

Before the House of Crimson Snow is a square glazed flower bed, in which mockorange trees are planted between rockeries. The mockorange was a native plant of Sichuan province. In 1823, upon order of the empress dowager, some mockorange trees that blossom with white flowers were transplanted to this flower bed.

In the southwest corner of the Imperial Garden is the Studio for Cultivating Nature. It faces east and has two stories with 15 rooms on each floor. During the reign of Qian Long, it served as a library where books collected from all over the country were kept.

To the northwest of the Hall of Imperial Peace is the Pavilion of Lasting Splendour, which is 15 meters high, three-bay wide with 2 stories. This was where the emperor and his ministers wrote poems while enjoying the beautiful scenery in the garden. Poems and inscriptions are on display.

Opposite the Pavilion of Lasting Splendour is the Shrine of Four Gods which was built in the Ming dynasty. West of the Hall of Imperial Peace is the Pavilion of Pure Felicity, and east of it is the Pavilion of Floating Green. They were all built in the Ming times on a single-arch bridge. Before the Pavilion of Pure Felicity is the Pavilion of Thousand Au-

tumns, and before the Pavilion of Floating Green is the Pavilion of Ten Thousand Springs. The Pavilion of Thousand Autumns used to be a small temple where a memorial tablet of Emperor Tong Zhi was kept in the late Qing period. The Pavilion of Ten Thousand Springs used to serve as a shrine where a portrait of Guan Yu, the divine guardian of the Qing dynasty, was worshipped.

A dozen pine and cypress trees in this garden with joined branches before the Hall of Imperial Peace are more than 400 years old. They were planted in 1535, when the Hall of Imperial Peace was rebuilt. A story goes like this: In the Warring States period the king of the Song state, took by force the wife of Han Ping, a royal attendant, and made her his own consort. Han Ping was sent to do hard labour and was killed by the king after the project was completed. His wife came to the funeral and jumped into the grave. The emperor buried the couple in seperate tombs, but not far from each other. The following year a tree grew out of each tomb. The upper branches of the two trees joined together with birds singing in them. In later days such trees became the symbol of steadfast love.

A pathway in the Imperial Garden arouses great interest among visitors. The one-kilometer-long path is paved with pebbles composing nearly 1,000 pictures and designs and snakes its way between bamboo groves, pines, cypresses, and flowering plants. When building such a pathway, the workers must first fix an outline with carved bricks or tiles according to pre-made designs. Then tiny cob-

ble-stones of various colours were inlaid into empty spaces. Finally the mortar made up of lime, glutinous rice and tong oil was filled in between the cobble-stones. The designs are rich and colourful, and cover a wide range of subjects. Some pictures reflecting the life of ordinary people are very amusing. One of them is "Henpecked Husbands", which depicts two henpecked husbands, one with an oil lamp on his head, kneeling on a wooden bench, the other with a bench on his head, kneeling on a wash board, both being beaten by their wives. Another man is riding by on a donkey, followed by his wife on foot. Feeling envious, the kneeling man asks, "Why is your wife so nice to you? You are riding the donkey while she is walking behind." The man answers, "You don't know the truth. She broke my leg when beating me last night. Now I have to ride the donkey to see the doctor."

The cobbled pathway, the pavilions, waterpools, towering trees and flowering plants in this garden are in perfect harmony, and this constitutes the unique features of the imperial gardens.

Six Eastern Palaces and Six Western Palaces

The Six Eastern Palaces and the Six Western Palaces are located on the two sides of the three rear palaces. They were the residences of the imperial concubines. With a surrounding wall each palace forms a compound of 2,500 square meters. The main halls stand in the middle and the side-chambers are in the east and west. Each palace has two courtyards. The hall in the front yard was used for formal audience, and the hall in the backyard served as the bed-chamber. Pine and cypress trees are grown in the front yard together with some flowering plants and miniature landscapes. A water well can always be found in each backyard.

The architecture of the 12 palaces are much similar, and they are connected by passageways which vary in width. The first north-south passageway is nine meters wide and the second is seven meters wide. There are six-four-meter-wide east-west alleys. At each end of the alley a glazed gate marks the boundary of each palace. All the buildings are well-planned and the architectural design is noted for ingenuity and originality.

The Six Eastern Palaces are situated on the east of the three rear palaces. They are Jingrengong (Palace of Great Benevolence), Chenqiangong (Palace of Heavenly Inheritance), Zhongcuigong (Palace of Quintessence), Yanxigong (Palace of Prolonged Happiness), Yonghegong (Palace of Eternal Harmony) and Jingyanggong (Palace of Great Brilliance). Behind the Six Eastern Palaces are five groups of buildings where young princes lived.

The Six Western Palaces are situated on the west of the three rear palaces. They are: Yowgshougong (Palace of Eternal Longevity), Yikungong (Palace of Assisting Empress), Chuxiugong (Palace of Gathering Elegance), Taijidian (Hall of Evolution), Changchungong (Palace of

Eternal Spring), Xianfugong (Palace of Universal Happiness). Behind the Six Western Palaces are five groups of buildings where young princes lived.

The Six Eastern Palaces and the Six Western Palaces are the residential areas for the imperial concubines of various ranks in the Ming and Qing times. The Qing empresses also lived in this area together with young princes and princesses. The number of imperial concubines varied from emperor to emperor. Jia Jing had the biggest number of concubines in the Ming dynasty. He had 59 concubines with official titles, whose names have been found in historial records, and innumerous concubines without titles. Emperor Kang Xi had the biggest number of concubines in the Qing dynasty. Altogether he had more than 100 concubines, of whom 39 were conferred upon official titles. Emperor Guan Xu had one empress and only two concubines, so he had the smallest number of concubines in the Qing dynasty.

Palace of Great Benevolence (Jingrengong)

Built under the reign of Yong Le in the Ming dynasty, it was first called "Palace of Long Tranquility" and renamed "Palace of Prospect and Benevolence" in the reign of Jia Jing. The present building dates back to 1655 when it was rebuilt under the reign of Shun Zhi of the Qing dynasty. A marble screen opposite the palace gate is said to be made in the Yuan dynasty.

Shun Zhi's empress, Tong Jia, lived in this palace. She was a concubine when she first came to the Imperial Palace. On May 4, 1654, she gave birth to Prince Xuan Ye (Emperor Kang Xi) at the age of 15. She died on March 20, 1663 when she was only 24.

The empresses of Yong Zheng and Jia Qing all lived in this palace. Guang Xu's favourite concubine Zhenfei also lived here.

Zhenfei was the daughter of vice-minister Chang Xu. In 1888, Zhenfei, at the age of 13, was chosen as a concubine together with her 14-year-old sister. Next year she was appointed the concubine of fourth rank and was promoted to the third rank in 1894.

Zhenfei was pretty and virtuous. She was fond of poetry and good at painting. Liao Jiahui, a court artist gave her much help in improving her skill. Usually she lived in this palace, but she often stayed with the emperor at the Hall of Mental Cultivation owing to Guang Xu's special favour. This naturally invited jealousy on the part of Empress Long Yu, who was the niece of Empress Dowager Ci Xi and often spoke ill of Zhenfei before her aunt. At that time the struggle between the faction headed by Empress Dowager Ci Xi and that headed by Emperor Guang Xu was becoming more and more acute. Zhenfei showed strong support for the emperor's political ideas, and consequently made Ci Xi bristle with anger. Zhenfei was beaten up and demoted to the 5th rank. On the 1st day of the 11th lunar month of the 20th year of Guang Xu's reign, Ci Xi issued an edict: "The empress has the responsibility to take charge of the concubines in the six palaces. Anyone who does not abide by the domestic discipline, interferes with state affairs, or confounds right and wrong will be subject to severe punishment. The empress should watch out for any misconduct and give me a true report on such cases. Grave panelty will be inflicted upon the offender with no lenience whatsoever." All this indicated that Ci Xi persecuted Zhenfei not only because of the contradiction between the mother-in-law and the daughter-in-law, but more importantly because of political reasons.

Having accepted the proposal on reform which was brought up by Kang Youwei and other reformers, Emperor Guang Xu issued an imperial decree on June 11, 1898 to carry out reform on a national scale in an attempt to keep the Qing dynasty from declining. This made Ci Xi hot with rage. On September 21, 1898, Ci Xi launched a coup detat and executed the six leaders of the reform movement. Guang Xu was put under house arrest at Yingtai, Zhongnanhai. Zhenfei was kicked out from this palace and jailed in many different places. After Ci Xi had moved to the Hall of Happiness and Longevity, Zhenfei was confined to a small courtyard not far from her residence.

Palace of Heavenly Inheritance (Chengqiangong)

It was first built under the reign of Yong Le in the Ming dynasty, and rebuilt three times afterwards. Formerly it was called "Palace of Eternal Benevolence". The present name was given under the reign of Chong Zhen, the last emperor of the Ming dynasty.

Lady Tian, a favourite concubine of Chong Zhen lived here. Her father Hong Yu was a vice-governor. Delicate, reticent and versatile, she married Chong Zhen when he was a prince. In the first year of Chong Zhen's reign, she was appointed the concubine of the third rank, and then promoted to the first rank. She gave birth to the fifth prince, Zhu Cihuan, and died in the 15th year of Chong Zhen's reign.

In the Qing dynasty, Shun Zhi's favourite concubine Dong E lived in this palace. A native of Manchu, she was the daughter of a minister, and brought into the palace at the age of 18. In 1656 she was first appointed concubine of the third rank, and then promoted to the first rank. Nominally Lady Dong E was inferior in position to the empress, but she had won favor of Emperor Shun Zhi and had in fact taken the place of the unsuccessful empress. Shun Zhi intended to force the empress to abdicate and install Lady Dong E as the new empress. However, he was foiled in his attempt owing to the strong objection from Empress Dowager Xiao Zhuang. In 1660 Lady Dong E died, and her coffin was placed in this palace. Shun Zhi was in such grief that he kept on wailing and even wanted to commit suicide. The royal attendants had to keep watch on him day and night. He then astounded everybody by declaring that he was going to be a monk and had already found a Buddhist name for himself. On the day of Lady Dong E's death, Shun Zhi gave the order that all the princes, officials above the 4th rank, princesses, concubines, and the wives of the officials above the third rank assemble at Jingyun Gate to pay their last respect to her and express their deep sorrow for her death. Court audiences were suspended for five days. On the third day, Lady Dong E was promoted to be the empress posthumously. A ceremony to mark the promotion was held in this palace. On the 5th day, the emperor wrote a long panegyric on Lady Dong E. He also instructed one of the court scholars to write her biography. Upon his order more than 30 eunuchs and palace-maids were killed and buried in Lady Dong E's tomb. All the officials throughout the country had to wear mourning apparels for a month and the civilians for three days. Lady Dong E was only 21 when she died. Since her death Emperor Shun Zhi had sunk into a morbid melancholy. In less than six months he died of small pox at the age of 24.

Lady Nala, a concubine of Emperor Dao Guang had once lived in this palace. She was, at first, only a palace maid, and promoted to be a concubine after she gave birth to Prince Yi Wei. Lady Wu Ya, another concubine of Dao Guang, also lived in this palace for some time. She began her court life as a low-ranking concubine and ended up as a concubine of the second rank because she gave birth to three princes.

Palace of Quintessence (Zhongcuigong)

It was first built under the reign of Yong Le in the Ming dynasty and rebuilt in the 12th year of Shun Zhi's reign. In November 1577, the front hall was renamed the Hall of Rising Dragon and the rear hall the Hall of the Sages. A small courtyard in the back was called the Studio of Imperial Virtue.

When Emperor Tai Chang of the Ming dynasty was the crown prince, this palace was his residence. In the Qing dynasty Prince Yi Zhu lived here for 17 years.

On the eve of a grand ceremony, the emperor always kept a fast at the Palace of Fast, whereas the empress always performed a fast in this palace. The empress of Dao Guang once lived here. Empress Dowager Ci An moved to this palace from the Hall of Physical Harmony after Tong Zhi was married. She was appointed the concubine of the 4th rank in 1852 and subsequently became the empress. After Tong Zhi was enthroned, Empress Dowager Ci Xi and Empress Dowager Ci An held court behind the curtain in the Hall of Mental Cultivation. In 1869 An Dehai, a court eunuch, left Beijing on a trip to the south, where he was supposed to inspect the making of imperial robes. However, on his way he blatantly sought publicity and extorted money from local officials, so he was arrested by Ding Baozhen, governor of Shandong province, and later executed upon the order of Empress Dowager Ci An. In 1873 Emperor Tong Zhi began to assume the reins of government. In 1874 he died. After his death Guang Xu succeeded the throne and the two empress dowagers resumed the old practice of holding court behind the curtain, as the new emperor was only four years old. In 1881 Ci An died a sudden death in this palace at the age of 45 and was buried in Zunhua, Hebei province.

Guang Xu's Empress Long Yu lived in this palace. She was the daughter of Ci Xi's brother Guei Xiang and designated as the empress in 1888. Ci Xi's designation of her niece as the empress was clearly aimed at controlling the emperor and consolidating her power. In the first lunar month of the 15th year of Guang Xu's reign, Long Yu was carried into the Imperial Palace in a palanquin escorted by royal guards of honor. On the 27th day of the same lunar month, Guang Xu and Long Yu were formally married. On the following day the empress was crowned in the front hall of this palace. All the imperial concubines, princesses, the wives of royal family members and high-ranking officials came here to extend their greetings to her.

Palace of Prolonged Happiness (Yanxigong)

It was first built under the reign of Yong Le of the Ming dynasty and rebuilt under the reign of Kang Xi and Xian Feng of the Qing dynasty. It was called the Hall of Longevity in the early Ming times and given the present name during the reign of Jia Jing.

The rebuilt palace was once called the Crystal Palace during the reign of Xian Feng. In the first year of Xuan Tong's reign it was turned into a water palace with water pools surrounding it and all the windows paned.

According to the chronicle of the Qing dynasty the Crystal Palace stood in the center of the compound with glass walls and glass floors supported by a bronze structure. Water was filled in between the glass walls and underneath the glass floors so that the emperor and the empress could see fish swimming amid water plants in the glass walls and in the pool under the glass floors.

Some of Dao Guang's concubines had lived in this palace for some time.

Palace of Eternal Harmony (Yonghegong)

First built in the reign of Yong Le of the Ming dynasty and rebuilt in the 25th year of Kang Xi's reign, it was called the Palace of Eternal Tranquility in the early Ming times and renamed at the end of the Ming dynasty.

In the Ming dynasty this palace was occupied by the imperial concubines of the second rank. In the Qing dynasty Lady Wu Ya lived here. On December 13, 1678 she gave birth to Yin Zhen (Emperor Yong Zheng). She was just a concubine of the fourth rank in the 18th year of Kang

Xi's reign and promoted to the third rank in the 20th year. After Yin Zhen was crowned as emperor she became the empress dowager. On July 25, 1723 she died in this palace at the age of 64.

Jingfei, a concubine of Dao Guang, lived in this palace. She began her court life as a concubine of the 5th rank, and gradually made her way up to the third rank. In 1832 she was promoted to the second rank after giving birth to the 6th son of the emperor. Having borne the emperor three sons and one daughter she ended up as a concubine of the first rank. In the 20th year of Dao Guang's reign, the empress died. Jingfei took over the responsibility of rearing Prince Yi Zhu, the 10-year-old son of the deceased empress. She showed more concern and love for Yi Zhu than for her own children. Prince Yi Zhu regarded her as his dear mother. After Yi Zhu ascended the throne with the reign title Xian Feng, he conferred an honorific title on her to express his gratitude to her for having brought him up.

Lady Fu Chai, a concubine of Tong Zhi, lived in this palace. She was brought into the Imperial Palace at the age of 14. At first Empress Dowager Ci Xi planned to make her the empress, but Empress Dowager Ci An disagreed, so she was appointed a concubne of the 3rd rank and later promoted to the first rank.

The rear hall of this palace was called Tong Shun Zhai (the Studio of Unity and Harmony), where Jinfei, a concubine of Guang Xu, had lived. She was born in 1875 and was selected as an imperial consort together with her sister Zhenfei. She was first appointed a concubine of

the 4th rank and then promoted to the third rank, but soon demoted to the 5th rank because of her sister Zhenfei. In the 21st year of Guang Xu's reign she regained her position as a concubine of the third rank. In 1923 she died and was buried in Yi county, Hebei province.

On the east wall of this palace is a calligraphy by Liang Shizheng, and on the west wall is a painting by a court artist. Both the calligraphy and the painting described the following story: Fanji was a concubine of King Zhuang of Chu state during the Spring and Autumn period. King Zhuang ruled from 613 to 591 B.C. For some time he spent too much time hunting. Fanji tried in vain to stop him doing that so she refused to eat the meat of animals or birds. Eventually the king turned a new leaf and worked hard on government affairs.

Palace of Great Brilliance (Jingyanggong)

It was first built in the reign of Yong Le of the Ming dynasty and rebuilt in 1686.

In the Ming dynasty Empress Xiao Jing, the mother of Emperor Tai Chang, lived in this palace. She was only a royal attendant when she was first brought into the Palace of Benevolence and Tranquility at the age of 17. Emperor Wan Li happened to see her while he was visiting his mother, the empress dowager, in that palace. He slept with the girl and she became pregnant soon. In those days whoever in the palace slept with the emperor

would, as a rule, get some reward. The royal secretary also kept a record of the date and the gift given to that girl, which could be used in the future as the proof of such relation to the emperor. Nevertheless, Emperor Wan Li tried to cover up the affair. One day the empress dowager inquired about it while he was dining with her. When he denied the inglorious act, she ordered the attendants to bring the record to the table and showed it to him. Then she softly said, "I am getting old and still haven't got any grandson yet. If she gives birth to a son, it will mean great happiness for our imperial clan. As the saying goes, a humble mother will enjoy a high social position if the rank of nobility is conferred on her son. Why do you look down upon her?" In 1582 Wan Li appointed the girl Gongfei, a concubine of the third rank. Not long after that, Gongfei gave birth to Zhu Changlo, the first son of the emperor, who was appointed the crown prince in 1601. However, Gongfei didn't get any promotion until the crown prince had his first son in the 34th year of Wan Li's reign, when she was promoted to a concubine of the first rank. Because of the power struggle within the royal family, it was difficult even for the crown prince to see his mother, and such visits were always under close watch. Only with the approval of the emperor could the crown prince come to see her in his palace. The palace gate was locked and the prince had to open it with a key. Having become blind, she could only feel him up and down, and said with tears, "My dear son, you have grown up, healthy and strong. I'll have no regret when I die."Gongfei lost her freedom only because she used to be an attendant. She died of sorrow in the 39th year of Wan Li's reign and was buried in the royal cemetery. Ten years later her son Zhu Changlo ascended the throne in 1620 with the title Tai Chang. He gave the order that his mother be promoted posthumously to the rank of empress dowager. However Zhu Changlo had ruled for only 29 days at the time of his unexpected death. Then his son Zhu Youxiao succeeded the throne. He carried out his father's unfulfilled wishes and his grandmother's coffin was reburied at Ding Ling just by the side of the coffin of Emperor Wan Li.

The rear hall of this palace served as the Imperial Study, where Kang Xi studied when he was the crown prince. A plaque with an inscription in Qian Long's handwriting "the Hall of Learning Poetry" was hung on the wall. During the reign of Qian Long the poems written by Emperor Gao Zong of the Song dynasty and the illustrations by Ma Hezhi to these poems were stored in this study, hence the name of the hall.

Twelve paintings made upon the order of Qian Long were also kept in the study. These paintings portrayed empresses or imperial concubines of ancient times for their exemplary conduct. Every year they were hung in the east and west palaces at the same time as the New Year couplets were pasted on door panels. They would be brought back and stored in this palace again in the second lunar month the following year.

Palace of Eternal Longevity (Yongshougong)

It was first built under the reign of Yong Le of the Ming dynasty and rebuilt in the Qing dynasty. In the earlier days it was called the Palace of Lasting Joy and renamed under the reign of Wan Li.

In the Ming times, Jifei, a concubine of Emperor Chen Hua, lived here. Jifei was a native of Guangxi. The expeditionary forces sent to Guangxi by Chen Hua killed her father, the chief of a local tribe, and took her captive. Because she was very intelligent and had had some schooling before, she was sent to the Imperial Palace, where she worked as a librarian. One day Chen Hua looked round in the stack-room and saw the girl. The emperor fell in love with the girl at the first sight and brought her to his bedchamber. The news that she was pregnant came upon Lady Wan, the emperor's favourite concubine, with a great shock. Lady Wan was from Shandong. She was at first a palace-maid serving the grandmother of Chen Hua, and later became the chamber-maid for crown prince Zhu Jianshun. Lady Wan was already 35 years old when Prince Zhu was enthroned at the age of 16 with the reign title Chen Hua. Although she was senior to the emperor by 19 years, she still managed to win his favour continuously, and was soon promoted to be a concubine of the third rank. As she was very smart and good at catering to the emperor's every wish. In 1466 Lady Wan gave birth to a son, so she was promoted to the second rank. But unfortunately her son didn't live longer than 100 days. Her wishful thinking to control both the emperor and his successor vanished just like soap bubbles. Therefore she was filled with hatred and anger when she learned that Lady Ji, the ex-librarian, was pregnant. She ordered a palace maid to force Lady Ji to take aborticide. However the maid was sympathetic with Lady Ji and detested Lady Wan. She lied to Wan that Lady Ji was seriously ill. So Wan ordered that Lady Ji be moved out of the Forbidden City and stay at An Le Tang (the Hall of Peaceful Joy), where the sick palace-maids were recuperating. On July 30, 1470 Lady Ji gave birth to Prince Zhu Youtang. It was said that owing to the effects of the aborticide, part of the prince's scalp was permanently bald. Lady Ji asked Zhang Min, a eunuch, to drown the new-born baby for fear that the secret might be revealed to Lady Wan. Zhang Min was shocked, saying, "His Excellency has not got a son, how can you throw it away?" So he and the deposed Empress Wu secretly raised the baby at Zhongnanhai for as long as six years. One day in 1475 Zhang Min was combing the emperor's hair. Chen Hua, looking at himself in the mirror, sighed, "I'm getting old but still haven't got a son." On hearing this, Zhang Min prostrated himself on the floor, saying, "I ought to be condemned for keeping Your Excellency in the dark. Your Excellency has got a son." The emperor was stunned at his words and asked where. Zhang answered, "I am telling the truth at the risk of my life. Your Excellency should protect the prince from falling a prey to any plot." Huai En, another eunuch, broke in, "What Zhang Min said is true. The prince is being cared for at Zhongnanhai, and he is six years old now." The emperor was overjoyed at the good news and ordered the royal attendants to bring over the prince. Lady Ji held the young prince tightly in her arms, crying, "How can I live on without you, my dear son." Then she told her son, "If you see the man with beard dressed in yellow robes, that's your father." Prince Zhu Youtang was carried into the palace and the emperor held up the prince in his arms and looked at him for a long time. He said excitedly, "It is my son. He looks just like me." On the following day the emperor instructed the cabinet to issue an imperial decree to the whole country in celebration of this happy event. Lady Ji was promoted to be a concubine of the second rank and moved to this palace. But in the 6th lunar month that year, she died suddenly and eunuch Zhang Min committed suicide. In the 11th lunar month the same year, Zhu Youtang was appointed the crown prince and put under the care of the empress dowager. However Lady Wan had not abandoned her mean intention and often invited the crown prince to visit her palace. Before he left, the empress dowager always warned the prince not to eat any food offered to him. Therefore when Lady Wan urged him to eat, the prince refused, saying, "I'm afraid it is poisonous." Lady Wan was so infuriated that she fell fatally ill and died soon after. On September 22, 1487 this crown prince ascended the throne with the reign title Hong Zhi.

In 1590 Emperor Wan Li lived in this palace. In 1638 Zhu Youjian (Chong Zhen), the last emperor of the Ming dynasty, kept a fast in this palace because natural calamities were frequently seen during his reign.

Palace of Assisting the Empress (Yukungong)

It was first built under the reign of Yong Le of the Ming dynasty and rebuilt in 1655 under the reign of Shun Zhi of the Qing dynasty. It was called the Palace of Ten Thousand Peaceful Days in the early Ming times. Emperor Jia Jing renamed it the Palace of Assisting the Empress, which was meant imperial concubines should assist the empress in every way they could.

Emperor Xuan De of the Ming dynasty bestowed a gold seal upon Lady Sun, his favourite concubine, who lived in this palace, and set a precedent for concubines owning gold seals. In 1428 Empress Hu was deposed and Lady Sun, a concubine of the second rank, was promoted to be the empress. After her son was crowned as Emperor Ying Zong, she became the empress dowager. When Ying Zong was held captive in the war against the northern invaders, his brother Zhu Qiyu took over the reins of the government upon the order of Empress Dowager Sun.

Lady Yuan, a concubine of Emperor Chong Zhen, lived in this palace. In 1644 when the peasant uprising troops led by Li Zicheng were about to enter the city, the emperor ordered Lady Yuan to commit suicide by hanging herself. But the string snapped and she fell in a dead faint on the floor. When she came arround, the emperor chopped at her shoulders with his sword, and wounded many other concubines.

In the Qing times the concubines of higher ranks lived in the central chamber, whereas those of lower ranks had to live in the side-chambers. In 1887 Empress Dowager Ci Xi lived here, and a grand ceremony was held in this palace to celebrate her 50th birday. In the late Qing dynasty a portrait of Ci Xi was hung in the east chamber and a portrait of Empress Xiao Zhe, the wife of Tong Zhi, was hung in the west chamber.

In the Ming times, on Qingming Festival officials and the ladies in the Imperial Palace were all appareled in silk, and concubines and the palace-maids stuck willow twigs in their hair. It was also called Swing Day by the people inside the palace. One swing was put up at the Palace of Earthly Tranquility and at each of the east and west palaces. The empress would start having a swing first at her residence and the ladies in other palaces would then follow suit. This custom was carried on in the Qing times. The iron rings under the eave of this palace were the remaining fixtures of the swing erected in the Qing times.

On the old site of the rear hall of this palace, the Hall of Displaying Harmony was built in 1802. It served as a dining hall when Ci Xi lived in the Palace of

Gathering Elegance. In those days breakfast was served at 6:30 a.m., lunch at 12, dinner at 6 p.m., and refreshments were served at any time she wished. According to Tang Guanqing and Chen Pingshun, two former eunuchs, and De Ling, the personal attendant of Ci Xi, more than 50 kinds of staple food and 120 courses were prepared for each meal; 250 kilograms of meat and over 100 chickens and ducks were consumed everyday and 450 attendants waited on Ci Xi at each meal. Before she started eating, an attendant would come forward and taste each dish to see if it was poisonous. A small piece of silver tablet, about one-inch long, was put inside each bowl as an indicator of poisoned food. When it was ready, the food was first put in specially designed boxes, which were made of wood and painted yellow with the design of two dragons playing with a ball. Each box had a hollow bottom made of tin, in which hot water was filled. Since each box was wrapped up in a cotton-padded covering, the food inside could be kept warm for quite a long time. At meal time, eunuchs filed along from the kitchen to the gate of the hall, food boxes in hand. Zhang De, one of the most trustworthy eunuchs, would take over the food boxes one by one and lay them down on the table. Ci Xi was seated before three square tables, facing the east. The food utensils included multi-color chinaware made in the royal kilns such as green bowls with yellow dragon design covered by silver lids, pink bowls with four characters meaning longevity, and some enamel ware. Ci Xi's favourite food was always placed closest to her. She ate only from a few dishes, and most of the food was simply for show. After she finished her meal the untouched food would be granted to the empress and the concubines, or sent over to the residences of Prince Chun, Prince Gong, Prince Qing, or other royal family members. The cost of one meal for Ci Xi was equal to that for 10,000 peasant families. Both the Palace of Eternal Spring and the Palace of Peace and Longevity had kitchens reserved exclusively for Ci Xi. Each kitchen was divided into many sections preparing different kinds of food, such as meat, vegetable, rice and bread, refreshment, roast food, etc. The cooks could make as many as over 10 varieties of porriage, over 100 types of refreshments, and more than 1,000 different delicacies.

In the 13th year of Guang Xu's reign, Ci Xi selected the empress and the concubines for the 18-year-old Emperor Guang Xu in this hall. Before the selection started, five girls from the families of high officials walked in as candidates for the appointment. They stood in a row in front of the empress dowager. At the head of the line was the daughter of deputy Marshal Gui Xiang, and also the niece of Ci Xi; in the middle were the two daughters of Governor De Xin of Jiangxi province; at the end were the two daughters of vice-minister Chang Xu in charge of protocol, Ci Xi was seated on the throne watching, and Guang Xu stood beside her. The princesses, female royal family members and the wives of high-ranking officials were standing behind the throne. In front of Ci Xi was a long table, on which were placed one jade Ruyi and two pairs of red embroidered pouches. According to the rule, the emperor would give the Ruyi to the girl whom he chose as his empress and give the pouches to the girl he chose as his concubine. Pointing at the girls, Ci Xi said to Guang Xu, "Now you may give the Ruyi to the girl you like best. It is you who make the decision." As she said this, she handed over the Ruyi to Guang Xu. But Guang Xu declined, saying, "This important matter should be decided by mother, not by me." However Ci Xi insisted he make his own choice. When Guang Xu went over to the daughter of De Xin and was about to give her the Ruyi, Ci Xi yelled, "Your Excellency!" and hinted to him that he should give it to her niece standing at the head of the line. Guang Xu was puzzled and handed over the Ruyi to the girl with reluctance. She was to become the empress and eventually the empress dowager. Ci Xi was aware that Guang Xu liked De Xin's daughter, and it was quite certain that the girl would snatch the emperor's favors from her niece. Before Guang Xu went on with the selection, she hastily ordered the princess to put the pouches in the hands of Chang Xu's two daughters. This was how the ceremony of selecting imperial consorts was concluded. Chang Xu's two daughters were brought into the palace the following year and were appointed concubines of the 4th rank one year later.

Palace of Gathering Elegance (Chuxiugong)

It was first built under the reign of Yong Le of the Ming dynasty, and renovated twice in 1655 and 1802. In the early days it was called the Palace of Longevity and Prosperity, then renamed under the reign of Jia Jing. In the Qing dynasty the empresses of Jia Qing, Xian Feng and Tong Zhi all lived in this palace.

In 1654 Emperor Tong Zhi was 17 years old. The two empress dowagers began to discuss the emperor's marriage. One candidate for the position of empress was 19-year-old Lady Alute, who was the daughter of Cong Yi, the Minister of Interior. The other candidate was 14-year-old Lady Fu Cha. The two empress dowagers were at odds on the question of who should be the future empress. Ci An chose Lady Alute, but Ci Xi thought Lady Fu Cha was an excellent choice. Ci An said, "Fu Cha is skittish and not suited to be the empress. She can only be a concubine of the 5th rank." As Ci Xi started as a concubine of the 5th rank herself, she naturally felt a sharp sting in Ci An's words. Since the dispute was locked in a stalemate, emperor Tong Zhi was summoned to their presence and they left him to decide who would be the empress. Tong Zhi followed Ci An's advice and chose Lady Alute as his empress and Lady Fu Cha as his concubine. Of course, Ci Xi was very unhappy about the emperor's choice. She put up innumerable obstacles in Alute's

way during the wedding ceremony. She also secretly ordered eunuchs to keep watch on her. Ci Xi was fond of operas. The empress had to keep her company at the theater inside the palace. During the show the empress always turned aside and faced the wall when there was a scene of obscenity on stage. Ci Xi repeatedly asked her to look at the stage, but she refused. When Tong Zhi was dying in his sickbed, Ci Xi insulted the empress openly before the eunuchs and the palace-maids. The empress, who was carried into the Forbidden City through the main entrance on the day of marriage, looked down upon Ci Xi, who, as a concubine of the 5th rank, came into the Imperial Palace through the back gate. Therefore the conflict between the mother-in-law and the daughter-in-law was getting more and more intense. Tong Zhi died on January 12, 1875. According to the tradition of the Qing dynasty, after the emperor died, the empress would become the empress dowager whether she was pregnant or she adopted a son to succeed the throne. Naturally it was the young empress who had the right to hold the court behind the curtain. Ci Xi, certainly, did not want things to happen that way. She refused to designate an heir to the throne from among Tong Zhi's nephews, as was traditional in those days. Instead she put Tong Zhi's 4-year-old cousin on the throne. By doing so, Ci Xi could still hold the court behind the curtain as the foster mother of the emperor. As to the young empress, Ci Xi intensified her persecution. She lived alone for three months and died a sudden death in this palace.

Ci Xi broke the long-established traditions of the Qing dynasty by taking up residence in this palace. In accordance with the rules set down by the early Qing emperors, the empress dowager should live in the Palace of Benevolence and Tranquility in the western Outer Court. Nevertheless, Ci Xi insisted on living here, because it was more convenient for her to go to the emperor's residence to hold court behind the curtain. Guang Xu lived in the Hall of Mental Cultivation during his childhood, and Ci Xi lived in the west-chamber beside it. After Guang Xu assumed the reins of government, Ci Xi moved to the Palace of Eternal Spring. The tenth day of the tenth lunar month of the tenth year of Guang Xu's reign was the 50th birthday of Ci Xi. She gave the order to renovate and redecorate the Palace of Gathering Elegance, the Hall of Displaying Harmony and the Palace of Assisting the Empress one year earlier for that occasion. All together 630,000 taels of silver was spent on the project. In order to celebrate her birthday in a big way, Ci Xi moved from the Palace of Eternal Spring to this palace in the tenth lunar month. Today the furniture and the decorations in this palace still look the same as on Ci Xi's 50th birthday.

This palace has a 5-bay space. Under the eave are paintings in bright colors, which depict various fairy tales. The doors and windows were painted with the motif of happiness and longevity. Of the six palaces, this one is the most exquisitely fitted up and most richly decorated. In the central hall there is a throne, on which are a spittoon made of lacquer ware and a Ruyi made of white jade. Two potted flowers made of green jade are placed on the stands beside the throne. A gilded peach-shaped incense-burner sits on each side. This hall was the place where Ci Xi received daily greetings. The birthday gifts given to her on her 50th birthday are put on display here. In front of the palace gate stand bronze dragons and deer, symbols of good luck. The four walls of the courtyard are inscribed with eulogies written by court scholars for the occasion of Ci Xi's 50th birthday.

More than 180 eunuchs and palace-maids waited on Ci Xi when she was living in this palace. It was not until 1894 that Ci Xi moved out to the Hall of Happiness and Longevity in the northeast corner of the Forbidden City in order to celebrate her 60th birthday.

When the last emperor Xuan Tong was in power, this palace was occupied by Lady Xun, one of the concubines of Emperor Tong Zhi. After he got married, the deposed emperor lived in this palace with his wife Wan Rong.

Further back is the rear hall, which was named the Room of Beautiful Scenery under the reign of Guang Xu. Inside it there used to be a small stage for local operas. A wooden carved armchair was placed in the middle to the east for Ci Xi to sit in while watching the show. A mirror of extraordinary size in the east wall served as a secret door leading to the side-chamber. Ci Xi lived here when she first came to the Imperial Palace as a concubine of the 5th rank. In 1856 she gave birth to Prince Zai Chun (Emperor Tong Zhi) in this room.

Ci Xi was born on November 29, 1875 in Changzhi, Shanxi province. At that time her father Hui Zheng was the county magistrate. Her childhood name was Little Orchid. The first year of Xian Feng's reign happened to be the year for the selection of Xiunü (candidates for imperial concubines). Little Orchid was among the successful candidates and was appointed the concubine of the 5th rank. She was brought into the palace the following year at the age of 16, and lived in the rear hall of this palace. In 1854 she was promoted to the 4th rank. On April 27, 1856 she gave birth to Prince Zai Chun, and for this was promoted to the third rank. In 1857 she was promoted to the second rank. In 1861 Emperor Xian Feng died in Rehe, and Prince Zai Chun succeeded the throne. Since then she had been addressed as Empress Dowager Ci Xi. She died in Zhongnanhai in 1908 at the age of 74. Many stories of how Ci Xi was picked up by the emperor have circulated among the people for generations. One of these goes like this: Lady Nala (Ci Xi) grew up in south China. She was pretty and intelligent. Apart from that she had a good voice and could sing ditties of the south beautifully. In the first year of Xian Feng's reign, she was selected to be a palace-maid in Yuanmingyuan Garden. One day while taking a walk in the garden, the emperor heard somebody singing a southern popular tune. He was deeply impressed, so he came to the place again the next day. As he was approaching the villa, the singing started. The emperor asked his attendants who was singing, and one said it was Little Orchid.

Then the emperor walked into the house and sat on the bed, saying, "Bring the girl here." After talking briefly to Little Orchid, the emperor ordered her to sing the song again out in the veranda. After a while, the emperor asked her to serve tea. When she brought the tea in, the other attendants all walked away. The emperor slept with her and she gradually won his favor ever since.

Hall of Evolution (Taijidian)

It was first built under the reign of Yong Le in the Ming dynasty and rebuilt in 1683. The present name was given under the reign of Kang Xi in the Qing dynasty.

Lady Jun, a concubine of Emperor Chen Hua of the Ming dynasty, lived in this hall and gave birth to Zhu Youyuan, the 4th prince. In 1487 this prince was granted the title Prince Xin and in 1491 he was appointed the governor of Anlu prefecture, Hubei province. His son later succeeded the throne with the reign title Jia Jing. In 1596 Emperor Wan Li moved to this hall, because there had been a fire in the Palace of Heavenly Purity, his formal residence. During his stay in this place a three-panel screen was put in the front room. A map was drawn on the central panel, while a namelist of the civil officials and another one of the military officials were pasted respectively on the left and right panels just for the emperor's reference.

Lady Yu, a concubine of Emperor Tong Zhi, lived in this palace. She was at first of the 4th rank and subsequently promoted to the third rank. During the reign of the last emperor Xuan Tong, she was granted the title equal to empress dowager. In 1924 she was forced to leave the Forbbiden City and settled in a small lane in Beijing.

Behind it is Ti Yuan Hall (Hall of Vital State), which was built in the 7th year of Jia Qing's reign on the old site of the rear part of the Hall of Evolution. Ci Xi lived here for some time.

Palace of Eternal Spring (Changchungong)

It was built under the reign of Yong Le of the Ming dynasty and rebuilt in 1683. The name of the palace was given by the emperor to symbolize his ever-lasting rule.

In the Ming times, Empress Hu, the wife of Xuan De, lived in this palace. In 1417 she was chosen as the concubine for Prince Zhu Chanji. She was crowned as the empress upon the coronation of Prince Zhu. However the emperor soon became fond of Lady Sun, a concubine of the second rank. To make the matter worse, the empress was in poor health and did not have any son. Two years later, the emperor ordered her to write a resignation and abdicate from the throne. She lived in this palace after her abdication.

Lady Li, a concubine of Emperor Tian Qi, lived here, too. She was persecuted by Wei Zhongxian, a powerful eunuch, and Lady Ke, the wet nurse of the emper-

or, and once stripped of her rank and titles. One day before the presence of the emperor she pleaded for mercy for Lady Fan, a concubine who had fallen into disfavour. Having learned about it, Lady Ke and Wei Zhongxian, who manipulated the emperor and interfered with state affairs, gave the order that Lady Li be locked in without food. Luckily she had learned a good lesson from those disfavoured concubines who died of starvation after the food supply was cut, and had stored some food, which was enough to last her for 15 days. After she was set free, Lady Li was reduced to palace-maid, and was compelled to live in an out-of-way place.

Lady Fu Cha, the empress of Qian Long, also lived in this palace. After she died, her coffin was kept here for some time. She was born on March 28, 1712 in the family of a provincial governor. Qian Long married 16-year-old Fu Cha upon the order of his father. In the second year of Qian Long's reign, she became the empress, and in the 13th year she went with the emperor on an inspection tour in east China. They visited the hometown of Confucius and held a memorial ceremony at the Confucian Temple. On their way back to Beijing, she died in Dezhou, Shandong province, and was buried in Zunhua county, Hebei province. Thirty thousand taels of silver was spent on her burial.

Lady Fu Cha was virtuous and courteous. Although she was the empress, she wore velvet flowers instead of jewelry or expensive hair-pins. She gave the emperor leather pouches she made out of deer skin, just as Manchu wives did in the old days. Since she had not forgotten the hard

life in the past and still kept up the fine tradition, she rapidly got into the good graces of the emperor. Qian Long was stricken with great grief at her death. He wrote a poem in memory of her and ordered that her palace be sealed off. On festive days her portrait would be put up in this palace for worship, and her crown, necklace and personal effects remained in the original place.

Emperor Tong Zhi assumed the reins of government soon after he was married. Empress Dowager Ci Xi moved from the Hall of Swallow and Happiness (Yanxitang) to this palace since it was no longer necessary for her to hold court behind the curtain. Five days before her 50th birthday (November 27, 1884), Ci Xi sat in the main hall here, watching an opera show together with princes, dukes, princesses and high-ranking officials' wives.

Shufei, a concubine of the deposed emperor Pu Yi, also lived in this palace. The side-chamber served as her study. On the surrounding walls of the palace is a mural "A Dream of Red Mansions", which was made under the reign of Guang Xu. In the mural the corridor was done in perspective to give the viewer an impression that the corridor is extending into far distance. This demonstrates the outstanding skill of the artist.

Palace of Universal Happiness (Xianfugong)

It was built under the reign of Yong Le of the Ming dynasty and rebuilt in

1683. Its first name was the Palace of Longevity and Peace, and its present name dates back to the reign of Jia Jing.

Lady Li, Wan Li's concubine of the second rank, gave birth to two princes, but she soon fell ill and then died after being treated by Zhang Ming, a eunuch serving Lady Zhen, another concubine of the same rank. The two princes were put in this palace under the care of Empress Xiao Duan who became their foster mother.

In 1799 Qian Long died, and his son Emperor Jia Qing came to this palace to observe mourning for his father. During this period of mourning, the emperor, instead of sleeping in a comfortable bed, slept on a straw mattress covered with a white blanket. The entire court went into mourning for 30 days. The emperor was not supposed to sleep on a bed until the end of this period, when a grand funeral ceremony would be held. Even after 30 days of mourning, the emperor would still have to handle affairs in this palace. This practice was carried on by both Dao Guang and Xian Feng.

The painting "Lady Feng Barring the Way of a Bear" and the calligraphy "In praise of Lady Feng" used to be hung on the east wall of this palace during the reign of Qian Long. Lady Feng Yuan was an imperial concubine of Western Han Emperor Yuan Di (reigned 48-33 B.C.). One day the emperor visited a zoo. a bear escaped and rushed to attack the emperor. Feng Yuan ran forward and stood in the animal's way. Her brave deed won the emperor's great respect, hence she was promoted to be the empress. Later on her

son was appointed Prince Zhongshan and she became Empress Dowager Zhongshan.

The rear hall is called Tongdaotang (Hall of Moral Order). It served as the dining room for Emperor Xian Feng. Manuscripts of two imperial decrees issued by Empress Dowager Ci Xi and Ci An in 1861 were kept in the files stored here. These manuscripts were all impressed with two small seals, which Xian Feng gave to Ci An and Tong Zhi, the child emperor, to authenticate official documents, shortly before his death. The two seals were used on imperial documents until 1873, when Tong Zhi took over the reins of government. The manuscripts of the two imperial decrees found in this hall indicated that Ci Xi and Ci An had handled state affairs in this place. After Tong Zhi died, this hall was turned into a storehouse.

Studio of Pure Fragrance (Shufangzhai)

It was built under the reign of Qian Long in the shape of "工". A small room to the east was where Qian Long prepared his lessons when he was the crown prince. The rear hall served as a dining room, where Qian Long had breakfast together with his mother. Tong Zhi and Guang Xu followed his example by keeping Ci Xi and Ci An company at meal time. In the back of the studio there is a small indoor stage. Performances were given here while the royal family banquet

was in progress. Qian Long himself played the fiddle for his mother to show his filial piety.

After Qian Long retired, he gave banquets here to entertain both Manchu and Mongol princes, dukes and marquises. Xian Feng, Tong Zhi and Guang Xu had all held royal family banquets in this studio.

Traditionally on lunar New Year's Day, the emperor would write such Chinese characters as "Happiness" or "Longevity" of extra-large size in his own style of calligraphy and then give them to the empress, the concubines, the royal family members or the ministers, just to show his favour towards his subjects. This practice could be traced back to the reign of Kang Xi, who wrote "Happiness" with an exceptionally large writing-brush. From then on the other emperors all followed his example. Yong Zheng, Qian Long, Jia Qing, Dao Guang, Xian Feng, Tong Zhi and Guang Xu also wrote "Happiness" as New Year gifts to their subjects. On that day the princes, dukes, ministers and the court scholars had to wait quietly outside the Gate of Heavenly Purity. Then they would file in, kneel down before the emperor's desk and kowtow before taking the paper with a big character "Happiness".

In the front yard of the studio, there is a theater stage with four columns on each side and a large opening in the ceiling. Theatrical performances were put on here on festive days, such as the lunar New Year's Day or the birthday of the empress dowager. On these occasions a long string of palace lanterns with beautiful tassels hung from each of the winged roof at the front of the stage.

On festive days the emperor would come here to enjoy theatrical performances after receiving congratulations or greetings from royal family members and high-ranking officials. The princes, dukes and the ministers were also permitted to watch the show together with the emperor. Although Qian Long had retired, he still came here from time to time for opera shows. As the father of Emperor Jia Qing, Qian Long was seated in the porch of the studio just opposite the stage, whereas Jia Qing had to sit in front of the side chamber. The ministers had to kowtow to the emperor once before they were seated, and were offered some food during intermission. After the performance ended, they had to kowtow to the emperor three times before they left.

The Qing court had a special department in charge of theatrical and musical performances. In those days the actors were usually the court eunuchs who had received some training in the royal opera school. During the reign of Guang Xu the eunuchs working in the Palace of Peace and Longevity organized an opera troupe and gave professional performances. In addition to that, local opera troupes were often called to put on Beijing opera in the palace. Some best-known actors in those days, such as Tan Xinpei, Chen Delin, Mei Lanfang, Yang Xiaolou and Jiang Miaoxiang had all been summoned to perform for the royal couple and their family members. The opera show always started between 6-7 o'clock in the morning and ended at 5 or 8 o'clock in the afternoon.

The actors were rewarded as much as 1,000 taels of silver for each performance. In 1922 when Pu Yi, the deposed emperor, was married, operas were staged for three days in a row at a cost of more than 30,000 yuan.

Palace of Double Glory（Chonghuagong）

The front hall of this palace is called the Hall of Happiness and Kindness. Its name on the horizontal board was written by Qian Long when he was the prince. There are some Buddha statues and two gold pagodas in the side chambers. The pagodas made of solid gold measure 4.6 feet high and weighs 2,480 ounces each.

This palace used to be the residence of Qian Long after he was married at the age of 17. Shortly after he ascended the throne, Qian Long renamed it the Palace of Double Glory. He gave family banquets here in honour of the empress dowager. In the first lunar month every year, Qian long and Jia Qing would hold banquests here to entertain the ministers and court scholars. On such occasions the table for Qian Long was placed in the central hall, and the table for Jia Qing in the side-chamber. During the banquet, Qian Long, the retired emperor, and his son Jia Qing always composed some poems together with the ministers. Sometimes tea parties were also given in this place. In the early days of Qian Long's reign, the number of guests invited to the banquets varied from time to time. In the 31st year of Qian

Long's reign, the number was fixed at 18. On lunar New Year's Day, Qian Long, though retired, received the greetings from his sons and grandsons in the front hall of this palace, and the greetings from the concubines, princesses and princes' wives in the rear hall.

Palace of Exuberant Happiness（Jianfugong）

To the west of the Six Western Palaces is the Hall of Prolonged Celebration. Every year on the day of "the Beginning of Spring" the emperor came to this hall for the Ceremony of Welcoming Spring, at which the emperor bowed nine times and prayed for the happiness of his people. Farther north is the Palace of Exuberant Happiness, before which stands Wu Chen Hall built in 1740. Banquets were given here every year in honour of visiting Mongol princes, dukes and marquises who had come to pay homage to the emperor. The palace used to be a part of the royal housing area in the Ming dynasty. Emperor Qian Long converted it into a palace to spend his leisure time in. In the spring of 1746 Qian Long accompanied his mother to look around the flower garden here and then had dinner together. He found this place was cooler than his own residence, the Hall of Mental Cultivation, so he intended to move to this palace. However he refrained from bringing this matter up before his mother.

The tablet for Empress Xiao De, the first wife of Xian Feng when he was the prince, was placed in this palace. She died in 1839 and was appointed posthumously the empress after Xian Feng came to the throne. The portrait of Empress Dowager Ci An was hung here for worship and Guang Xu came to this palace to make an obeisance to her. According to Miss Liu, former palace-maid, Zhenfei, the favourite concubine of Guang Xu, was jailed here after the 1898 coup.

Behind the palace is Huifeng Pavilion built in 1740. The petrified wood and cloisonne vats inside it are all left from the Ming times. There is also a large piece of brown-colored jade, 1.8 feet high and 2.1 feet wide, which sounds like bronze when struck with hand. It is inscribed with calligraphy by a number of well-known scholars.

The Western Garden at the back of this palace was built in 1740 with an area of 4,000 square meters. This place used to be another part of the royal housing area in the Ming dynasty. Qian Long made the decision to convert it into a garden, where he could relax.

In the late Qing dynasty the buildings near this palace became treasure houses, where gold Buddha statues, gold pagodas and the portraits of the Qing emperors were stored. The old paintings and rare curios Qian Long liked were sealed up and kept in a building near the garden after his death at the order of his son Jia Qing. In 1922 the deposed emperor Pu Yi wanted to know the exact number of his treasures, so it was decided that an inventory be made of all the storehouses. But the check-up had just begun when a fire broke out on the night of June 27. All the

antiques and rare curios stored here were burned up and the unique garden was reduced to ashes. The art treasures destroyed in the fire included a Tibetan Buddhist sutra, up to 1,000 gold Buddha statues and gold musical instruments used in Buddhist service, four gold pavilions, several thousand blocks of Tibetan Buddhist sutra carved during the reign of Jing Tai of the Ming dynasty, and a huge gold pagoba in the Hall of Justice and Rectitude, which measured 16 feet high and was made of 11,119.9 taels of gold under the reign of Yong Zheng.

The garden close to the Palace of Exuberant Happiness used to be one of the four royal gardens in the Forbidden City, but it is different in design from the Imperial Garden and Ci Ning Garden which are characterized by symmetrical layout. The area was not a good place for building a garden, for the land was flat and surrounded by the high walls of the palaces in the vicinity. The artisans overcame these unfavourable conditions by constructing winding corridors connecting the buildings and tall mansions against the high walls. The garden was not only elegant, but also rather peaceful and secluded. Qian Long loved to stay here in his spare time. The construction of the garden behind the Palace of Tranquility and Longevity was based on the plan of this garden. Of all the royal gardens built on the palace grounds, this one is the most extraordinary because of its unique style in architectural design.

Palace of Abstinence (Zhaigong)

The Palace of Abstinence is located south of the Six Eastern Palaces. It was first built in 1731 and renovated in 1796. The ancient tradition required the emperors of both Ming and Qing dynasties to worship Heaven and pray for good harvest in the Temple of Heaven on winter solstice. Three days before the winter solstice, the emperor had to leave the Imperial Palace and stay in the Palace of Abstinence in the Temple of Heaven, where he was supposed to eat no meat, have no contact with women, drink no wine, have no merry-making and be concerned with no legal matters. The emperors of the Ming dynasty, Shun Zhi and Kang Xi of the Qing dynasty all went to the Palace of Abstinence in the Temple of Heaven three days before the ceremony of Worshipping Heaven was held. Nevertheless, since Yong Zheng was crowned as the third emperor of the Qing dynasty, this traditional practice was partially changed. Although Kang Xi, Yong Zheng's father, had quelled down the San Fan rebellion, anti-government uprisings still broke out from time to time around the capital or in the other parts of the country. After Yong Zheng came to power, there was a bloody fight between the emperor and his brothers who had some sworn followers. He feared that he might be in danger of being assassinated if he stayed in the Temple of Heaven alone. So he decided to build another Palace of Abstinence inside the Forbidden City, which was also called Neizhai(the Inner Palace of Abstinence). Consequently the one in the Temple of Heaven was called Waizhai (the Outer Palace of Abstinence). For three days before the ceremony, Yong Zheng stayed in Neizhai, and on the eve of winter solstice he left the Forbidden City late at night and stayed in Waizhai for a few hours before he attended the ceremony. In other words, the old tradition existed only in name, and the Palace of Abstinence in the Temple of Heaven had virtually become a place for rest.

Hall of Mental Cultivation (Yangxindian)

Located south of the Six Western Palaces, the Hall of Mental Cultivation stands in the center of a large compound, 80 meters from east to west and 63 meters from north to south, with an area of more than 5,000 square meters. The gate to the front yard is called Zunyimen (the Gate of Righteousness). There are two back gates to the back yard. Entering the Inner Right Gate from the Outer Court, one comes to Xichang Street. Farther north is Zunyimen, beyond which are some small rooms for the eunuchs or guards on duty. Farther west used to be the office of Wong Tongsu, Emperor Guang Xu's teacher. In the middle of the north wall is the Gate of Mental Cultivation, in front of which are two gilded bronze lions. South of the red wall oppo-

site the gate was the royal kitchen and its southern warehouses.

This hall was first built in the Ming dynasty and rebuilt under the reign of Yong Zheng of the Qing dynasty. Shaped like the letter "I", it has totally 12 rooms. However, there are 20 rooms in the extensions of the rear hall.

The purpose this hall served in the Ming dynasty can not be found in historical records. But judging from its name and location, we deduce that it was an auxiliary building attached to the Palace of Heavenly Purity, the emperor's formal residence. In the early Qing dynasty Emperor Shun Zhi took up his residence in this hall, and died here on February, 5 1661. During the reign of Kang Xi this hall became the office for the Works Department of the Imperial Board. In order to show his filial piety, Emperor Yong Zheng moved to this hall and observed mourning for his father for as long as 27 months. From then on, the other Qing emperors all lived in this hall.

In the main room of the front hall hangs a horizontal board bearing the Chinese characters for "Just and Benevolent" in Yong Zheng's handwriting. These words were meant to remind his successors of the importance of formulating a correct policy in ruling the country. The testaments of Qian Long, Jia Qing and Dao Guang are hung up on both sides of that board. In the centre of the coffered ceiling is a sculpture of a dragon playing with a huge pearl. The imperial throne is placed on a low platform in the middle of the room. Behind it is a rosewood screen engraved with a poem composed by Qian

Long in 1760 after his army put down the rebellion of Dzungarians, a Mongolian tribe. At the back of the throne are two small doors leading to the rear hall. On both sides stand some bookcases made of red sandalwood. During the reign of Kang Xi, a celestial ball was put on the east side of the throne, and a large globe was put on the west. Eighteen sets of the imperial edicts signed by the emperors are placed on a long table to the east, and the book the *History of Imperial Dynasties*, an enamel tripod, a jade burner and a vase are placed on the table to the west. In the second year of Guang Xu's reign, red sandalwood-framed wall panels with gold bamboo design hung on the east and west walls.

In this hall Emperor Yong Zheng bestowed food on his subjects, and Qian Long gave audience to the successful candidates of the imperial examination in the main room on June 9, 1736. It was used as a banquet hall on the lunar New Year's Day in the third year of Jia Qing's reign. In the Qing dynasty the emperor granted audience to officials and summoned his ministers for consultation in the central hall. The officials who were to be promoted, transfered or whose tenure of office was to expire were presented to the emperor by the Minister of Interior. On this occasion the officials had to be on their knees before the emperor while making a detailed report of his antecedents. In 1797 Marshal Erledengbao brutally suppressed the uprising of Bailianjiao (the society of White Lotus) and in 1856 Minister Sungelinqing put down the uprising of Nian Army. To reward the two generals for their meritorious deeds, Emperor Jia Qing and Emperor Xian Feng respectively accorded them heart-warming receptions. In the feudal dynasties when the officials were received by the emperor, they had to bow three times and kowtow nine times. But these two men were exceptions. As the emperor and the general met in the reception hall, they held each other's arms, which was a very special honour in the feudal society.

A horizontal board with an inscription and a couplet, both written by Yong Zheng, are hung on the north wall of the west warm chamber. The inscription reads: "Diligent in handling state affairs and respectful to the talented". The couplet says that Heaven assigned the mandate of the country to one person, but did not demand the whole populace to serve one person. To the north is a couch, and the emperor's desk stands by the royal seat. This room served as the emperor's office, where he read memorials, conferred with his ministers or went through the test papers of the ten scholars who came out top in the imperial examination. Here Jia Qing once granted an audience to Kong Qingrong, the 73rd generation posterity of Confucius, and planned the suppression of the uprising of Tianlijiao (Society of the Nature's Law). "Quotations from Emperor Qian Long of the Great Qing Dynasty" are placed on a long table close to the west wall. During the reign of Qian Long a namelist of the provincial governors, county magistrates, generals, etc. were put up on the west wall for the emperor's reference.

The west warm chamber was where the emperor read and wrote. In 1746 it was renamed Sanxitang (Room of Three Rarities), because three samples of calligraphy by Wang Xizhi, Wang Xianzhi and Wang Xun, famous calligraphers of the Jin dynasty (265-420) were kept here. It is eight square meters in area and elaborately decorated. The floor of the outer room is paved with blue tiles. In the inner room there is a bed covered with a yellow blanket and a yellow embroidered mattress. The east wall is inlaid with colourful vases. On the west wall is a painting by Jin Tinbiao, a court artist, which depicts how the well-known calligrapher Wang Xizhi taught his son Wang Xianzhi the calligraphy skills. Qian Long was noted for his lavish patronage of classics and works of art. He often took great delight in looking at paintings and calligraphy in this room. He had a special seal carved, which bore Sanxitang, the name of this studio, and applied the seal to every piece of graphic arts he liked. Besides he scoured everywhere for art treasures and then enjoyed fondling them here. But he ordered that 538 kinds of books, 13,862 volumes in all, be burned in the pits built under the floor for winter heating, because he thought these books were detrimental to the rule of the Qing dynasty. A wooden wall was built outside the west warm chamber as a security measure to prevent eavesdropping or peeping in.

In the east warm chamber of the front hall, there is a platform close to the south window with a low table on top. Every year the ceremony of writing the first article in a new year was performed at 12:15 p. m. on the lunar New Year's Day, when the emperor, dressed in ceremonial robes, sat at the low table on the platform and wrote "World Peace" and "Happiness and Longevity" to usher in an auspicious new year. After that the emperor would write a poem which was to be hung in this room later on. When the ceremony came to an end, the writing brushes, the lanterns, the gold goblet and other things used during the ceremony would be put in the storeroom, so that they could be used again the next year. This ceremony was first started by Yong Zheng and then carried on to the reign of Xian Feng. During the ceremony the emperor drank Tusu wine made in the royal kitchen, with the gold goblet as a preventive against illness. The platform in this chamber was dismantled under the reign of Tong Zhi, because the entire room had to be rearranged for the two empress dowagers to hold court behind the curtain. Emperor Xian Feng died on August 22, 1861. His six-year-old son suc- ceeded to the crown with the reign title Tong Zhi. Ci Xi, the child emperor's mother, became the empress dowager in spite of the fact that she was only a second-rank concubine. She and Ci An, Xian Feng's empress, declared, in the name of Emperor Tong Zhi, that the eight ministers who had been given regentship by Xian Feng, were guilty of treachery and treason. The two empress dowagers repudiated the last decree of Xian Feng and ordered that Su Shun be executed, Zai Yuan and Duan Hua commit suicide, and the other five ministers be removed from office and then exiled. In the tenth lunar month, Ci Xi sent somebody to the British Embassy to find out whether Britain would support her usurpation of the supreme power. She also instructed two ministers, Jia Zhen and Zhou Zupei, to whip up public opinion demanding her holding court behind the curtain. Some scholars edited a collection of past examples in the Chinese history of how empress dowagers handled state affairs on behalf of the emperors under age. When everything was settled, Ci Xi and Ci An proclaimed to the whole country on the first day of the 11th lunar month that they would hold court behind the curtain. This is known as the 1861 Coup in history.

Holding court behind the curtain means that the child emperor was seated on the throne in front, while the two empress dowagers were seated on the large throne behind. There was a yellow gauze curtain between the two thrones. Everything was decided by the empress dowagers sitting behind the curtain. This practice continued until Tong Zhi was married at the age of 18. On January 12, 1875 Tong Zhi died in the Hall of Peace Companion at the age of 19. After the death of the emperor, instead of adopting a son as Tong Zhi's heir to the throne, Ci Xi went against the long-established tradition of the Qing dynasty by appointing four-year-old Zai Tian, who was her sister's son and Tong Zhi's cousin, as the successor to the throne with the reign title Guang Xu. By so doing she could hold court behind the curtain again as the emperor's foster mother. On April 8, 1881 Ci An died unexpectedly and Ci Xi seized the power into her own hands as she was the only person sitting behind the curtain de-

ciding everything. When Guang Xu was married at the age of 19, she nominally gave up her authority. But in reality Guang Xu was only a puppet, because Ci Xi still pulled the strings behind the scenes. After the 1898 Reform was foiled, Guang Xu was put under house arrest at Yingtai, Zhongnanhai, and Ci Xi held court behind the curtain for the third time until 1908 when she died at the age of 74. The yellow gauze curtain on display in the east warm chamber today is a reproduction made after the design and size of the original one dating from 1881.

During the 47 years she was in power, the Qing dynasty was decaying rapidly. For many times she directed Zeng Guofan, Li Hongzhang and Zuo Zongtang to build up a modern army equipped with western rifles to suppress the people's uprising. With her approval the Qing government signed many treaties of national betrayal and humiliation with foreign countries. She not only sought power and wealth by betraying the country, but also preached the theory "to win the favour of the western powers with China's wealth". Her mismanagement of the government plunged the nation's existence into peril and brought great suffering to the Chinese people.

On November 14, 1908 Guang Xu died at Yingtai. Shortly before her death, Ci Xi made the decision that Pu Yi, the son of Guang Xu's brother Zai Feng, would be the heir to the throne with the reign title Xuan Tong, and his father would be the Prince Regent, who was responsible to bring up all important civil or military affairs to Empress Dowager Long

Yu for ruling. However the 1911 Revolution broke out and the provinces declared independence one after another. Xuan Tong issued an imperial edict under which the ban on political parties was lifted and the Royal Cabinet was dissolved. In addition to that, the emperor reinstated Yuan Shikai to command the Imperial Army and Navy, and launch a fierce offensive against the revolutionary army. In the mean time, Yuan was also instructed to form a Cabinet with himself as the Premier, and Zai Feng, the Prince Regent resigned his regentship. Counting on the military strength of the Qing government, Yuan, on the one hand, forced the revolutionaries to make compromise and negotiate peace. On the other hand, he took advantage of the surging revolution to coerce the Qing emperor into abdicating the throne. Empress Dowager Long Yu summoned cabinet meetings before the emperor one after another, but the princes held divergent views on the question whether to fight to the end or to negotiate peace. At this moment 42 generals under the command of Yuan Shikai demanded the Qing emperor to vacate the throne. Since there was not much to be done, the emperor was compelled to authorize Yuan Shikai to negotiate the conditions for his abdication with the Republican Army. The talks between the representatives of the South and those of the North began at the City Hall in the British Concession in Shanghai at 2:30 on the afternoon of October 28, 1911. After much consultation the representatives of the South and the North reached agreement on the preferential treatment offered to the Qing emperor in exchange for his abdication. Both sides signed the agreement which would end the rule of Qing dynasty for good. The northern representative was Tang Shaoyi, the plenipotentiary of Yuan's cabinet, and the entourage included Ou Genxiang, Xu Dinglin, Feng Yitong and Zhao Chunnian. Headed by Wu Tingfang and Wang Zhengting, the delegation of the South included Wen Zongyao, Wang Chonghui, Wang Zaoming and Niu Yongjian. On February 12, 1912 in the name of Emperor Xuan Tong, Empress Dowager Long Yu personally affixed the imperial seal to the Imperial Edict of Abdication in the east warm chamber of the Hall of Mental Cultivation, and formally declared that the emperor agreed to renounce the throne. The 1911 Revolution put an end to the feudal monarchy which had lasted several thousand years in China.

However, the deposed emperor still lived inside the Forbidden City. In June 1917 Zhang Xun led "the troops with pigtails" into Beijing and strongly supported Pu Yi's attempt at restoration. On July 1st the same year, the last emperor mounted the throne again in the Hall of Mental Cultivation and planned to regain his authority over the government. On July 12, the Republican Army entered Beijing. Their airplanes dropped three small bombs. One came down just off Long Zong Gate; one fell in the waterpool of the Imperial Garden, and one hit the eaves of Long Fu Gate near the Western Palaces. The offensive launched by the Republican Army quickly finished off the farce of restoration, which lasted only 12

days. On the morning of November 1924 General Lu Zhonglin, Zhang Bi and Li Yu under the command of Marshal Feng Yuxiang drove Pu Yi out of the Forbidden City.

The rear hall served as the emperor's bed-chamber. According to the records made in the second year of Tong Zhi's reign, as many as 720 art objects were set out in the bedchamber, including a framed wall panel with a jadeite-inlaid peacock design and a jade tray engraved with Qian Long's poem. The emperor's bedchamber is composed of the east bedroom and the west bedroom. The beds are covered with red and yellow blankets. The embroidered quilts, mattresses and draperies were all made in Nanjing, Suzhou and Hangzhou. On the bed-curtains are hung perfume pouches from Suzhou and Hangzhou. On the bed-curtains are hung perfume pouches of various colours. There was a silver nightstool with soft seat in the toilet to the west end of each bed.

The bed in the east bedroom was reserved exclusively for the empress when she came to stay with the emperor for the night. Over the front bed curtain is a horizontal board bearing the Chinese characters for "A new day comes". Close to the south window is a plat-form, on which stands a square table with a chessboard on it. On the east wall hangs a couplet made of enamel. The bed in the west bedroom was used by concubines when they came here at the call of the emperor. On the west wall hangs a calligraphy by Dao Guang. It contains a nine-character inscription that reads: "Willow waiting for the coming of the spring breeze", each

character consisting of nine strokes. Beginning from the winter solstice, he wrote one stroke each day and took nine days to finish one character. When all nine characters were done, spring came to replace the cold winter. This would be repeated the next year and soon became a customary practice in the Imperial Palace.

On February 17, 1799 Qian Long died in this hall. After he fell ill, his son Emperor Jia Qing looked after him here until his death. In 1874 the two empress dowagers summoned the princes and the ministers for a conference in the west warm chamber, at which they announced the decision to put Zai Tian, son of Prince Yi Huan, on the throne as the successor to Tong Zhi with the reign title Guang Xu. On the same day Guang Xu was brought into the palace through the Great Qing Gate and was shown to the two empress dowagers here in this hall.

East of the rear hall is the Hall of Manifesting Obedience, which was the temporary residence of the empress. After the emperor and empress were married, they first stayed together in the Palace of Earthly Tranquility for two days. On the third day, the emperor moved back to the Hall of Cultivating the Mind and the empress moved to this hall. After she had stayed here for three months, the empress would move out to her permanent residence. This hall was renamed the Hall of Mutual Harmony in 1872 and renamed again on the eve of Guang Xu's wedding. The name of the hall on the plaque was in Ci Xi's handwriting. The small rooms along the veranda to the east were temporary lodgings for the concubines who came here at the call of the emperor. West of the rear hall is the Hall of Swallow and Happiness, where provisional accommodation was provided for the concubines on call.

Tong Zhi acceded to the throne at the age of six. Empress Dowager Ci Xi lived in the Hall of Swallow and Happiness and Empress Dowager Ci An lived in the Hall of Manifesting Obedience, so that the child emperor would be well cared for. Besides, it was very convenient for the two empress dowagers to hold court behind the curtain. After Tong Zhi was married, Ci Xi moved to the Palace of Eternal Spring and Ci An moved to the Palace of Quintessence.

Office of the Privy Council (Junjichu)

Office of the Privy Council is located by the Inner Right Gate not far from the Gate of Heavenly Purity. It was set up in 1729 and abolished in 1911. The office is a simple one-storey house, low and small in sharp contrast with the towering and magnificent palace buildings. Nevertheless it was the most important organ of the Qing government, responsible for issuing orders to the whole country.

At first the Privy Council was set up only to strengthen the unified command of military operations in the war against the minorities in Xinjiang in Northwest China. The Ming emperors used to handle government affairs in the Outer Court, but the Qing emperors conducted state af-

fairs in the Palace of Heavenly Purity or the Hall of Mental Cultivation. The office of the cabinet was located in the southeast corner of the Outer Court. Some urgent war communiques had to go through a lot of formalities before they were presented to the emperor by the cabinet. In order to learn the situation on the battlefield and find counter-measures as soon as possible, and also to prevent the military secrets from leaking out, the emperor gave the order that an office for the officials in charge of military affiairs be put up near the Hall of Mental Cultivation, so that the emperor could summon these officials for consultation about important military affairs at any time. In 1732 this office was formally named the Privy Council. In 1747 the wooden structure that housed the office was replaced by a brick building with yellow glazed tiles as we see today. In 1736 its name was changed to Premier's Office, but it was changed back the following year.

Initially, the Privy Council was only concerned with military affairs, and the cabinet dealt with other state affairs. But later on the Privy Council overrode the cabinet in power. The Privy Councillors were reliable princes or ministers hand-picked by the emperor himself. The number varied from emperor to emperor, ranging from three to six. The Privy Councillors were directly involved in the management of state affairs and the handling of confidential matters, such as drafting imperial decrees, offering advice to the emperor, appointing or removing officials, setting the examination paper for the imperial examination, and making in-

spection tours in the country as the Imperial Commissioner. The emperor arrogated all powers to himself through the Privy Council. Between 3-5 o'clock every morning the Privy Councillors came to their office. Between 7-9 a.m. they were summoned to the east or west warm chamber in the Hall of Mental Cultivation. With their knees on floor cushions, they listened to the instruction of the emperor and began to draft the edicts on the spot, or exited first and then asked the officials on duty to make the draft, which would be reviewed by the emperor before it was sent out to different parts of the country by the imperial post. The couriers on horseback carrying ordinary documents travelled at a speed of 250 kilometers or so per day. For urgent messages they could go as fast as 400 kilometers a day.

The Privy Council had a silver official seal made in 1732. In 1737 a new seal made of solid gold was cast, which was kept in the Inner Fileroom of the Palace of Heavenly Purity. The key to the seal box was held by the Head Councillor. Besides, a gold tablet, 2 inches long, half inch wide and 0.1 inch thick, inscribed with three Chinese characters for Privy Council, was worn by the official on duty. Whenever there was the need to set the seal to an official document, both the key and the gold tablet must be shown to the eunuch at the Inner Fileroom before the seal was taken out of the box.

Because the Office of the Privy Council was where important matters were handled and confidential edicts were drafted, everyday two censors assigned by the emperor, stood on the door-steps in rotation, keeping watch and ward. All the officials, civil or military, even princes and dukes were not allowed to hang about the place. The Privy Councillors must not chat with anybody else during office hours. Only with the special permission of the emperor could the high-ranking officials come to the office, where they were permitted to read the emperor's instructions or the memorials to the emperor. Sometimes they were summoned here and the Privy Councillors read out the imperial edicts to them.

Inside the office, just above the lintel of the entrance hangs a tablet with the Chinese characters for "Harmony-Permeated Room". On the east wall hangs another tablet with the inscription "Glad Tidings Come from Battlefield" in Xian Feng's handwriting. He wrote it in celebration of the victory after the Qing government quelled the revolution of Taiping Heavenly Kingdom. On the north wall is the 23 articles of Constitutional Monarchy published in 1908.

Outer Eastern Palaces
—Palace for the Supersovereign

Beyond the Jingyun Gate in the northeast of the Forbidden City stands a group of imposing palace buildings with a total area of 46,000 square meters. Architecturally, this group of buildings is independent of the other parts of the Imperial Palace; however the general plan is made exactly after that on the central axis, i. e. three big halls in the Outer Court and three palaces in the Inner Court. The Outer Court is situated in the south, where the retired Emperor Qian Long received festive greetings from high-ranking officials. The Inner Court in the north was the residence of the retired emperor and his empress. In the Ming times, the Palace of Benevolence and Longevity stood in this area, where the empress dowager and the concubines of the deceased monarch lived. On its old site, Kang Xi built the Palace of Tranquil Longevity for her mother. Later on Qian Long extended the buildings around that palace, so that he might live there after he resigned the sovereign authority. Qian Long ascended the throne at the age of 25. He promised he would renounce the throne in favour of his son (Emperor Jia Qing) after he had ruled for 60 years, because he didn't want to have his reign last longer than that of his grandfather Kang Xi (Kang Xi had ruled for 61 years). In the 37th year of his reign Qian Long began to prepare for his abdication, and the construction of the palaces for him to live in after he retired was started at the same time. By then, Qian Long was already over sixty years old, and he was not certain whether he would be able to reign over the country for 60 years. Therefore he prayed to God for his blessing. Even the names of the various buildings in this area manifested such aspiration for a long life. For example, the Hall of Joyful Longevity, the Hall for Fulfilling the Original Ideal, the Tower of Living Up to Expectations and the Room of Sustained Harmony were thus named. His wish came true in 1796, when Qian Long abdicated the throne at the age of 85 and his son succeeded him. How-ever, he claimed to be the supersovereign and still retained his power. He had never lived in this area. Sometimes he came here only for a pleasant tour.

Just off Xiqingmen, the main entrance to the Outer Eastern Palaces, there is a Nine-Dragon Screen opposite the Gate of Imperial Supremacy. The screen is 3.5 meters high, 29.4 meters wide and built of 270 glazed tiles in yellow, blue, white, purple, indigotic and green colors. The nine dragons are in different vivid postures, romping, swimming in billows or amid clouds. The appearance of the screen is both solemn and resplendent. Entering the Gate of Imperial Supremacy, one suddenly sees a large open space of more than 5,000 square meters with old pine trees scattered along the sidewalls. To the north of the courtyard is the Gate of Tranquil Longevity, beyond which extends a marble-paved passageway, 1.6 meters above the ground, six meters wide and 30 meters long with carved marble balustrades on both sides, Leading to a splendid and lavishly-decorated building—the Hall of Imperial Supremacy.

Hall of Imperial Supremacy (Huangjidian)

It was known as the Palace of Tranquility and Longevity when built by Kang

Xi as the residence of his mother. In the 37th year of Qian Long's reign, it was rebuilt into a magnificent hall with double eaves for holding official ceremonies after Qian Long retired. The entire building was modelled after the Hall of Supreme Harmony and the Palace of Heavenly Purity. The front hall was named the Hall of Imperial Supremacy, where Qian Long received congratulations from nobilities. The rear hall of the building retained the original name—the Palace of Tranquil Longevity. Inside, there is a water clock to the east and a chiming clock to the west.

On the first day of the first lunar month of the 60th year of Qian Long's reign, a grand ceremony was performed in the Hall of Supreme Harmony to retire the old emperor and crown the new emperor. At the ceremony Qian Long, then aged 85, personally handed over the imperial seal to his son, Emperor Jia Qing. An imperial decree was issued to the whole country to declare this power transfer. When it was over, Qian Long was carried to this hall and more than 8,000 aged officials headed by Emperor Jia Qing came over to extend their congratulations to the supersovereign. Qian Long was the last retired emperor in the Chinese feudal dynasties.

According to the traditional practice, the retired emperor should move out of the Hall of Mental Cultivation so to make room for the new emperor. But Qian Long did not do so, nor did he live a restful life in the Outer Eastern Palaces. He changed his decision to confer power upon his son and continued to conduct state affairs in the Hall of Mental Cultivation on the pretext of supervising the new emperor. Therefore, Jia Qing, the emperor in name only, had to go on living in Shuqing Palace. Qian Long gave two reasons for not moving out of the Hall of Mental Cultivation. First, he had lived there for 60 years, so it must be very hard to adapt himself to a new residence. Second, it was convenient for the princes and ministers to come for an audience if he lived close to the Gate of Heavenly Purity, the main entrance to the Inner Court. Therefore he had never resided in the Palace of Tranquil Longevity, which was located a good distance away, and eventually died in the Hall of Mental Cultivation.

On the fourth day of the first lunar month of the first year of Jia Qing's reign, Qian Long, the supersovereign, gave a grand banquet to entertain several thousand aged men at the Hall of Imperial Supremacy to mark the prosperous and peaceful life in the country. In that year every province brought in good harvest and the national treasury reported surplus. Thirty hundred old men were present at the banquet and 3,497 poems were composed during the banquet. In order to make the emperor's appearance more impressive and add to the joyful atmosphere, orchestras were disposed along the veranda of the hall and off the Gate of Tranquil Longevity. Altogether 800 tables were laid for the banquet. Inside the main hall, gold-dragon tables were set before the throne for Qian Long and his son Jia Qing. Besides there were 38 tables for princes, dukes, marquises and officials of the first rank; 366 tables were spread in the veranda for officials of the second rank and foreign envoys; 60 tables were put on both sides of the central passageway for officials of the third rank; 240 tables were placed on the right and left side of the marble terrace for officials of the 4th or 5th rank and Mongol guests, 200 tables were set out outside the Gate of Tranquil Longevity for officials of the 6th to 9th rank; and another 200 tables were laid outside the Gate of Imperial Supremacy for retired guards, soldiers, artisans and ordinary citizens. All such banquets held under the reign of Qian Long were arranged by Ah Gui who found favour with the emperor. The age limit for the guests was set as follows: 60 or older for officials above the third rank; 65 or older for officials under the third rank; 70 or older for the rest of the guests. The oldest guest who attended the banquet was Xiong Guopei, aged 106, from Anhui province.

Under the reign of Guang Xu, Ci Xi celebrated her 60th birthday here. The celebration cost 4,386,204 taels of silver, of which 600,000 taels was spent on the reconstruction of the Palace of Tranquil Longevity and the Hall of Imperial Supremacy. In the 30th year of Guang Xu's reign, foreign envoys were received here. After the death of Ci Xi and Long Yu, their coffins were laid in the Hall of Imperial Supremacy before burial.

Behind the Hall of Imperial Supremacy is the Palace of Tranquil Longevity. In the early days it was the rear hall of the Palace of Tranquil Longevity. When Qian Long rebuilt it in the 37th year of his reign, the name-plate hung in the front hall was moved back to this hall. Its architectural design was very similar to that of the Palace of Earthly Tranquility. To the east was the bedchamber and to the west was the sacrificial chamber with a wooden platform and some musical instruments for religious services. The retired emperor was supposed to perform sacrificial rites here in accordance with the tradition established by the founders of the Qing dynasty.

During the reign of Guang Xu, Ci Xi and Ci An often set banquets here for the ministers. From the 12th lunar month to the first lunar month of the following year, Ci Xi stayed in the Palace of Tranquil Longevity, reading books or playing cards. At times she asked eunuchs to read out classical poems to her. The house east of the Gate of Tranquil Longevity was the kitchen and the house on the west was the pharmacy. The side-chamber on the west of the Hall of Imperial Supremacy was the residence of Li Lianying, the eunuch chief, and the one on the east was the residence of Cui Yugui, the deputy chief.

The Hall of Imperial Supremacy and the Palace of Tranquil Longevity are the major part of the Outer Court for the retired emperor. The Inner Court is composed of three large halls in the middle: the Hall of Cultivating Nature, the Hall of Joyful Longevity and the Hall of Sustained Harmony; three buildings on the east: the Pavilion of Fluent Music, the Pavilion for Watching Performances and the Hall of Celebrating Longevity; and Qian Long's Garden on the west.

The Hall of Cultivating Nature was supposed to be the residence of the retired emperor. It is just a copy of the Hall of Mental Cultivation in architectural design. The west room of this hall is called the Room of Fragrant Snow. Inside was an immortal's cave built of quarts stone, where Qian Long sat meditating.

Hall of Joyful Longevity (Leshoutang)

Behind the Hall of Cultivating Nature is the Hall of Joyful Longevity. The name of the hall suggested that Qian Long intended to live a long life in ease and comfort. Therefore, a huge piece of jade carving entitled "Accumulated Verdancy on Mount Nanshan", was placed on the left side of this hall, which signified that the emperor's life was as long as the evergreen pine on Mount Nanshan. It was carved from one piece of jade weighing 1.5 tons and took four years to finish. The Jar of Sea of Happiness, another jade carving of extraordinary size, was set out on the right. Its name implied that happiness was as vast as the East Sea. It was also carved from one piece of jade weighing 2.5 tons, and also took four years to complete. In the rear part of the hall stands a gorgeous jade carving on a bronze base inlaid with gold and silver. It is 2.24 meters high and 0.96 meter wide, weighing 5 tons. It shows how Yu, founder of the Xia dynasty (21st-16th century B.C.), led people in harnessing the Yellow River. This is the largest piece of jade carving existing in China today.

The raw jade was mined in Xinjiang in Northwest China and the carving was done in Yangzhou. Mining, transportation and carving took ten years altogether.

In 1894 Ci Xi moved to this hall from the Palace of Gathering Elegance and celebrated her 60th birthday here. Six hundred thousand taels of silver was spent for that purpose. The west warm chamber was her bedroom and the central hall was her dining room. At mealtime, four tables were spread in a row before the royal seat. Ci Xi sat at the west end of the tables and Guang Xu at the northwest. The food served included delicacies from both land and sea. The dinner sets were made of gold, silver, jade and jadeite. At that time in Ci Xi's kitchen near the Palace of Tranquil Longevity, there were more than 1,500 pieces of dinner sets. The gold dinner sets weighed 5,816 ounces and the silver dinner sets 10,590 ounces. On August 15, 1900 the Allied Forces of the Eight Foreign Powers invaded Beijing. At five o'clock in the morning Ci Xi coerced Guang Xu into running away with her from this hall. They finally escaped to Xian.

North of the Hall of Joyful Longevity is the Hall of Sustained Harmony. Inside, a poem carved on the east wooden wall entitled "Western Expedition" by Qian Long tells how the Dzungarians, a Mongol tribe, were quelled in 1758. On the west wall is an essay "On Dispelling Erroneous Thoughts", also by Qian Long. sums up the experience of the expedition. There is a small theater stage in the western courtyard of the hall. Farther back is the Pavilion of Great Blessing. In the northern courtyard of this pavilion, there were three small rooms, where Zhenfei, Guang Xu's favourite concubine, was put under house arrest. She was pretty and virtuous with great interest in poetry and painting. Sometimes she was dressed in the emperor's clothes and walked around in the palace in the disguise of Emperor Guang Xu, or dressed like a eunuch to keep Guang Xu company in the Hall of Mental Cultivation. Ci Xi was very angry about it. She was later put under house arrest because she ardently shared Guang Xu's views of political reform. On the eve of her escape to Xian, Ci Xi ordered Cui Yugui, the eunuch chief, to push Zhenfei into a well near the Pavilion of Great Blessing, on the pretext that she might fall a victim to the invading foreign soldiers. It was subsequently called Zhenfei's Well.

After the death of Ci Xi, Jinfei, Zhenfei's sister, set up a memorial hall to Zhenfei with a one-meter-high wooden tablet just north of the well. Services were conducted there every fortnight.

Qian Long's Garden

Qian Long's Garden is located to the northwest of the Palace of Tranquil Longevity. It was an integral part of the Palace of Tranquil Longevity built for Qian Long to live in retirement, hence it was called the Garden of the Palace of Tranquil Longevity. It is over 160 meters long and 37 meters wide with a total area of 6,700 square meters. Because it was constructed under the reign of Qian Long, it was commonly known as Qian Long's Garden. The economic development of the Qing dynasty reached its peak at the time the garden was being built. By then Qian Long had made four inspection tours south of the Yangtze River, where he had feasted his eyes on the beautiful scenery in famous gardens. As he was very much keen on the landscape in the southern country, this garden is just the miniaturization of the well-known scenic spots in the south. The garden consists of four small courtyards and the decorations inside the main buildings are mostly centered on the theme of pine, bamboo and plum—three friends in winter. Artificial hills built with rocks are seen everywhere, and pines, cypresses and bamboo groves add great beauty to the garden. Qian Long came here on inspection tour when it was still under construction. The names for the buildings in the garden were all given by Qian Long. Names such as the Hall for Fulfilling the Original Ideal, the Tower of Living up to Expectations, the Rest-from-Work Studio, reflected Qian Long's early wishes. After the completion of the garden, he came here frequently to enjoy the scenery, write poems or practise calligraphy.

The front gate of the garden is called the Gate of Spreading Prosperity, beyond which is a rockery screen. Behind the screen is a courtyard surrounded by the House of Ancient Glory to the north, Pavilion for Seeking Pleasure to the west, and a Hilltop Terrace to the east. An old catalpa tree stands in front of the House of Ancient Glory. Qian Long believed the tree would bring good luck to his off-springs because it was once dead and then revived. West of the House of Ancient Glory is the Pavilion of the Rising Sun, which faces the east and greets the sunrise every morning.

The Pavilion for Seeking Pleasure is square in shape with a cup-floating duct inside. Wine cups floated along the winding 10-cm-deep groove cut into the rock floor. The water comes from a well near the front gate. Everyday two iron vats beside the well were filled up with water, which flowed through the aqueduct under the rockery into the pavilion, and then flowed out into the ditch. In allusion to an essay by a famous Jin dynasty writer Wang Xizhi, Qian Long named the pavilion Xishang—seeking pleasure during festival in the spring on river banks to cleanse away evil influences. Opposite the pavilion is the Hilltop Terrace. South of the terrance is another small yard with winding verandas. In the southeast corner is an artificial hill on which stands a small pavilion. To the east is a small house, which was once used as a shrine.

Behind the House of Ancient Glory is the Hall for Fulfilling the Original Ideal. It is composed of the main room to the north and two siderooms on the east and west. In the middle is a courtyard with a few old cypress trees and rockeries, where Qian Long and Jia Qing often took rest and wrote poems. He gave the name to this hall because he hoped to abdicate in favour of his son after he had ruled the country for 60 years. Things turned out just as he expected.

Farther on are more rockeries with caves and tunnels, leading to the Pavilion of Towering Beauty, where one gets a panoramic view of the palace buildings. To the west, between the Tower of Prolonged Interest and a cliff is a chasm a dozen meters deep. Looking up from here, one gets a view of a "strip of sky". To the southeast of the artificial hill is the Three Friends Room. Decorations inside are centered on the theme of pine, bamboo and plum—three friends in winter. The room was heated in winter by burning firewood in the brick pit under the floor. Looking through the windows, one can see pines, bamboo branches and plums sway in the breeze.

The Tower of Living up to Expectations is located in the north of Qian Long's Garden. Viewed from outside, it is a two-storey building, but inside it has three floors. Platforms for sitting can be seen everywhere. The staircase is so narrow that only one person is allowed to climb at a time. On the third floor the throne was set out to the north with a screen and two ornamental fans behind it. Looking from the balcony of this floor, one can see not only the palace buildings in the Forbidden City, but also the white pagoda in Beihai Park. It is known as the "Labyrinth" for its complicated network of identical partitions, winding corridors and numerous doors and passageways. At the end of every lunar year Qian Long held banquet in the tower to entertain his ministers, Manchu aristocrats and Mongol princes.

The Pavilion of Jade Conch stands on the main crest of the Hill of Taihu Rock in front of the Tower of Living up to Expectations. It is a plum-shaped structure with five pillars and five ridges. Because of its decorations related to the plum, it is popularly known as the Plum-Blossom Pavilion. The shape of the pavilion is very peculiar and rarely seen in other imperial gardens.

Just opposite the Pavilion of Jade Conch is the Flying Rainbow Bridge, leading to the Villa of Cultivating Harmony. Farther north is the Room of the Essence of Jade. Behind it is the Hall of Bamboo Fragrance. Not far from the hall is the Rest-from-Work Studio, which lies in the northernmost part of the garden. Its western chamber is connected with the Hall of Bamboo Fragrance by a concealed corridor. Inside the chamber there is a small theater stage surrounded on three sides by a bamboo hedge. During the reign of Qian Long, eunuchs, to the accompaniment of timbrels and three-stringed guitars, sang folk ballads on this stage for the emperor.

Many of the Qing emperors liked to have their residences with large gardens, hence particular attention was paid to the design and construction of various types of gardens within the palace grounds.

Pavilion of Fluent Music (Changyinge)

It is located east of the Hall of Cultivating Nature, just opposite Qian Long's Garden. Built in 1772, this pavilion is the largest theater in the Imperial Palace. The 21-meter-high structure has three storeies, each having its own name: Happiness (top), Nobility (middle) and Longevity (lower). Surrounded by 12 columns, the lower floor is nine times as big as an ordinary stage floor, with five openings located in the middle and four corners. After pulling the lid up, the actor could jump down to the basement through the opening and walk to the backstage. Under one of the five openings there is a water well, which can enhance the sound effects by resonance. A capstan was installed under every opening to lift the actors or the setting up to the first floor. In the opera "Gold Lotus from Underground", five big lotus flowers with five Buddha statues on top were raised slowly through the five openings from under the stage. The middle floor is smaller than the lower floor and the actors moved around only in the front part of the stage. The upper floor is even smaller than the middle one and the actors could only act under the eave. The design of the size of these three stage floors was based on the line of the emperor's vision. There is an opening in the centre of the ceiling of the lower floor, through which one can see the ceiling of the top floor. There are other two openings in the ceiling leading to the middle floor. Windlasses are installed on the top and middle floors to let the actors go down through the opening to the lower floor. When the play written specially for birthday celebrations was put on here, over 100 actors taking on different roles of immortals and deities appeared on the three floors at the same time. It was a quite spectacular sight when all the immortals and the deities were extending their birthday greetings to the emperor.

Theatrical performances were the most popular recreation in the reign of Qian Long and Guang Xu. In those days it was customary to have various kinds of shows on the emperor's birthday, winter solstice, lunar New Year's Eve or the day of the emperor's coronation. There are altogether nine theatre stages of different sizes in the Imperial Palace. The place for the show depended on the importance of the day and the type of the performance. Operas were put on at this pavilion only on important festivals, such as the lunar New Year's Day and the emperor's birthday. During the reign of Tong Zhi and Guang Xu, when Empress Dowager Ci Xi held court behind the curtain, opera shows were given here on this stage most frequently. Although she lived in the Palace of Gathering Elegance in the reign of Tong Zhi, and the Hall of Joyful Longevity in the reign of Guang Xu, she never missed one show in this theatre. In 1884 she celebrated her 50th birthday, which fell on the 10th day of the 10th lunar month. However, the celebrations already began on the 22nd day of the 9th lunar month. Beijing opera shows went on for seven days on end. From the 8th day to the 16th day of the 10th lunar month, performances were given respectively at this pavilion and on the stage in the Palace of Eternal Spring for nine days and nights. On her birthday, Ci Xi, accompanied by Guang Xu, Empress Long Yu, imperial concubines and the high-ranking officials' wives, came to the Pavilion for Watching Performances just opposite this stage. The play they watched on that day were written to eulogize the times of

peace and prosperity. Princes, dukes, marquises, ministers, provincial governors and generals came to the show by order of the emperor, and they all had to stand while watching the show. Throughout the night music filled the air and the entire theatre was brilliantly illuminated with more than 400 palace lanterns hanging along the veranda and gallery of the two pavilions. For Ci Xi's 50th birthday celebrations, the theatrical entertainment alone cost 110,000 taels of silver.

Besides the Pavilion of Fluent Music, theatre stages of similar size with three platforms were also built in the Summer Palace, Yuanmingyuan Garden and at the Imperial Summer Resort in Chengde.

Behind the Pavilion for Watching Performances is Xunyan Study, where Qian Long used to write poems. When Ci Xi lived in the Hall of Joyful Longevity, Guang Xu came to the study for a rest before going there to give his daily greetings to her. Farther back is the Hall of Celebrating Longevity, where the wife of Prince Chun, the daughters of Prince Gong and Prince Qing lived when they came to the palace to keep Ci Xi company. Prince Chun's wife was Ci Xi's sister and also the mother of Guang Xu. Prince Qing was the seventh son of Dao Guang. His two daughters were often summoned to the palace. The fourth daughter was very smart and always found favour with Ci Xi. She never missed one opportunity to please the empress dowager. If Ci Xi showed love for a sleeveless jacket of certain style unintentionally, in less than three days the jacket would be presented

to her just in the style she liked. Prince Qing's promotion to Foreign Minister had a lot to do with the fact that his two daughters were close courtiers of Ci Xi.

North of the Hall of Celebrating Longevity is the Palace of Great Happiness, which was built in 1689 by Kang Xi for Empress Dowager Xiao Hui. It was a copy of the Hall of Joyful Tranquility in the garden of the Palace of Retained Happiness. This palace was reconstructed in 1772 and 1790 under the reign of Qian Long.

At the back of the Palace of Great Happiness is the Pavilion of Buddhist Glory, built against the surrounding wall of the Forbidden City. To the west is the Pavilion of Buddhist Sun. These two pavilions are so close to each other that they share the same flight of stone steps. The Pavilion of Buddhist Sun is a two-storey building with verandas on the outside. Inside, a portrait of the founder of the Yellow Sect of Lamaism and 10,900 small Buddha statues were put up for worship.

Outer Western Palaces
—Palace for the Empress Dowager

West to the Longzong Gate are the Outer Western Palaces. Located in the northeast corner of the Forbidden City, this group of buildings centers around the Palace of Motherly Tranquility with the Palace of Longevity and Health to its west, and the Palace of Longevity and

Peace to its north. These palaces were the residences of the empress dowagers and the imperial concubines of the deceased emperor. South of the Palace of Motherly Tranquility is a large garden of 6,400 square meters in area, which was called the Garden of the Palace of Motherly Tranquility and specially built for the empress dowager. North of the Palace of Motherly Tranquility are the Pavilion of Raining Flowers, the Hall of Treasured Flowers, the Hall of Justice and Rectitude, and the Hall of Brilliant Flowers, all of which served as Buddhist temples or shrines, where the empress dowager expressed her sorrow and prayed for health.

In line with the tradition of the feudal times, when the empress and the imperial concubines of his deceased predecessor still lived in the Six Eastern or Western Palaces, the new emperor of both the Ming and the Qing dynasties was not supposed to move in. There-fore, as soon as the old emperor was buried, his empress and concubines had to move out of the six Eastern and Western Palaces and took up their new residences in the Palace of Motherly Tranquility.

In the Ming dynasty, in addition to the Palace of Motherly Tranquility the empress dowager and the concubines of the deceased emperor also lived in the Palace of Benevolence and Longevity in the northeast corner of the Forbidden City, and the Palace of Benevolent Celebration in the southeast corner. In the Qing dynasty, the empress and the concubines of the deceased emperor lived in the Outer Western Palaces and the Palace of Tranquil Longevity. In the late Qing times, Empress Dowagers Ci Xi and Ci An lived in the Eastern and Western Palaces within the Inner Court.

Palace of Motherly Tranquility (Cininggong)

In front of the Gate of Motherly Tranquility are two gilded bronze lions sitting on stone bases. Beyond the gate is the stone-paved central passageway leading to a marble terrace, on which stand four gilded tripod incense burners, bronze tortoises and cranes. Besides there is one sundial and one moondial. the Forbidden City is the only place where a sundial and a moondial placed together. The palace building was first put up in 1536. Empress Dowager Li, mother of Emperor Wan Li, once lived here. In 1654 it was renovated by Emperor Shun Zhi of the Qing dynasty. Empress Dowager Xiao Zhuang, his mother, took up her residence in it. Because she was of Mongol nationality (Intermarriage between the Manchu and the Mongol noble families were common in those days), the nameplate hung over the gate is inscribed in Han, Manchu and Mongol languages.

Born in a noble's family, Xiao Zhuang used to be a concubine of Huangtaiji. During her entire life, she had assisted two emperors under age, and was directly involved in the government administration. Any decision related to important state affairs must first get her approval before being carried out. After Huangtaiji passed away, power struggle arose in the royal family owing to his failure to appoint his successor before his death. Xiao Zhuang seized the power for her six-year-old son Fu Ling by strategy. Whenever he made an important decision, Kang Xi always asked Xiao Zhuang for advice. Subsequently, with the support of Xiao Zhuang, Kang Xi prevailed over all opposing views and resolutely put down the San Fan rebellion. Obviously Xiao Zhuang had made important contribution to the unification of China in the Qing dynasty. She lived in the palace of Motherly Tranquility and died there at the age of 75.

The Palace of Motherly Tranquility was the main residence of the empress dowager, who received greetings here on the occasion of festive celebrations. In order to show his filial piety, Qian Long held grand ceremonies in this palace to celebrate his mother's birthday. In the 34th year of his reign, for celebrating his mother's 80th birthday, double eaves were added to the palace building so that it looked more imposing than before. The project cost 5,478 taels of silver.

The empress and the concubines of the deceased emperor lived an extravagant life in this palace. The empress dowager, in particular, enjoyed the best treatment in terms of not only etiquette, but also the daily expenditure.

There are many temples and shrines in these buildings. Because these old ladies lived an idle life, everyday they spent a lot of time praying for longevity and happiness in the next world. In the Buddhist shrines, coiling incense smoke could be seen and chanting of Buddhist sutra could be heard all day long. These aged empress dowagers and concubines were bored, so they were looking for spiritual sustenance in the imaginary Buddhist world.

In the Qing dynasty, people believed in such religions as Manchu Salmanism, Taoism, Confucianism, Buddhism, and Lamaism of which the Yellow Sect was the state religion. At that time the people in Tibet and Mongolia all believed in Lamaism. In order to pacify the people in these two regions, the emperor exalted the importance of lamaism. However, the emperor himself never worshipped the Buddha. He only paid a visit to the shrine occasionally and looked at the Buddhist statues with reverence.

Pavilion of Raining Flowers (Yuhuage)

It was first built in the Ming dynasty and reconstructed under the reign of Qian Long. The building is elegant in structure and unique in style. The second and the third storeys have extended eaves covered with blue and green glazed tiles. The tower at the top has a hipped roof covered with gilded bronze tiles with four gilded galloping dragons on the four ridges. Buddhist statues were put up inside the pavilion for worship and Buddhist mass was often held in it.

Hall of Magnificent Flowers (Yinghuadian)

Built in the Ming dynasty, it is located north of the Palace of Longevity and Peace. Buddhist statues were put up inside for worship. Various kinds of food was offered here as sacrifice all the year round.

In the Ming dynasty, the empress dowager and the empress always attended Buddhist service in this hall. Emperor Wan Li's mother planted two bodhi trees in front of the hall. people believed that it was under a bodhi tree Sakyamuni, the founder of Buddhism, came to enlightenment. Now these bodhi trees are about seven meters high. Their weeping branches touch the ground and they bear golden flowers in summer.

Gate of Divine Prowess (Shenwumen)

It was built in the Ming dynasty as the north gate of the Forbidden City. Its gate tower is 31 meters high. Formerly called Xuanwumen, the name was changed to avoid the character Xuan, for Emperor Kang Xi's name was Xuan Ye.

When the empress and concubines went to attend the ceremony of starting silkworm breeding every year, they always left the palace through this gate. The concubines chosen by the emperor were brought into the Forbidden City also through this gate. In the first year of Shun Zhi's reign, the empress dowager decreed that women with bound feet entering this gate should be executed. The decree was then put up inside the gate.

On March 19, 1644 the peasant uprising troops led by Li Zicheng broke the Forbidden City. Chong Zhen, the last emperor of the Ming dynasty, fled the palace through this gate and then hanged himself on Coal Hill. In the Qing dynasty, Xiunü (pretty girl) were chosen every three years from among the daughters of officials of the eight banners (military and administrative organization). The selection of palace-maids was made every year. All the girl candidates got off their carts at this gate and then walked to the Imperial Garden, where they would be interviewed. These girls, if chosen, would work in the palace until 25 years of age, unless they were picked as concubines of the emperor or the wives of the princes. Some girls left the palace through this gate ahead of time because they were either too clumsy or too sick to work in the palace anymore. If a girl had won certain rank, her aged parents could, by special permission of the emperor, come into the palace through this gate to see her.

The gate tower contained a bell and drum. Everyday at dusk the bell would toll 108 times. After that the drum would beat to sound the hour at each watch of the night until the bell again sounded 108 times at sun rise. The bell would not be struck while the emperor stayed in the palace.

East Flowery Gate (Donghuamen)

It is the east gate of the Forbidden City. The gate tower is 33 meters high. When officials went to court or came back from work, they always entered or left the Imperial Palace through East or West Flowery Gate. Two stone tablets, about four meters high, one meter wide, stand in front of the gate, one on each side. Each tablet is inscribed on both sides with "Dismount" in Manchu, Mongol, Han, Hui and Tibetan languages. Civil officials had to get off their palanquins and military officials had to get down from their horses on this spot. Then they went into the palace on foot.

There were 18 guards and five officers on duty at this gate, armed with shotguns and 16,840 arrows.

In the Qing dynasty the emperor's coffin was carried out of or into the Forbidden City through this gate.

West Flowery Gate (Xihuamen)

This gate has a 33-meter-high gate tower, inside which cotton-padded armors used to be stored.

In the Qing dynasty the empress dowager returned to the Imperial Palace from the Garden of Joyful Spring always through this gate. In 1752 in order to celebrate the 60th birthday of Qian Jong's mother, the ten-kilometer-long street from this gate down to Gaoliang Bridge outside Xizhmen city gate was decorated with lanterns and coloured streamers. Makeshift stages for performances were put up along the road to give a variety of shows when the royal procession was passing by. When Empress Dowager Ci Xi returned to the Forbidden City from the Summer Palace on her 70th birthday, Emperor Guang Xu awaited her arrival on his knees at this gate.

There were the same number of guards here as at the East Flowery Gate.

The Eunuchs

The eunuchs were castrated men employed in the imperial court. The origin of the eunuchs is associated with sterilization as a form of punishment in ancient China. In the Zhou and Qin dynasties, criminals, who had been neutered, were often sent to work in the court as servants, so as to avoid sexual promiscuity. Besides the emperor, princes and officials of the first and second rank were also permitted to employ a number of eunuchs to work in their residences.

Eunuchs almost always had something to do with the rise and fall of a dynasty. Because they were the closest to the emperor the eunuchs sometimes usurped the power and turned the emperor into a puppet. Following are some of the most powerful eunuchs in history. Zhao Gao of the Qin dynasty; Gao Lishi of the Tang dynasty; Tong Guan of the Song dynasty; Pu Buhua of the Yuan dynasty; Wang Zhen, Wang Zhi, Can Jixiang, Liu Jing and Wei Zhong-xian of the Ming dynasty; Li Lianying and Xiao Dezhang of the Qing dynasty. Emperor Zhu Yuanzhang, founder of the Ming dynasty, and Emperor Shun Zhi of the Qing dynasty had a special iron plate made and hung in the palace, admonishing the eunuchs not to interfere with government affairs. On July 16, 1923 the last emperor Pu Yi dismissed the last batch of court eunuchs in Chinese history. With the downfall of the feudal soeiety, the employment of eunuchs ceased to exist in China.

Selection of Eunuchs

Before they were permisted to enter the palace, the prospective eunuchs had to undergo a physical examination. In the Qing dynasty the Ministry of Rites was responsible for recruiting eunuchs. The candidates were first examined by veteran eunuchs with two officials from the Personnel Department observing. Then the head of the General Administration of the Royal House made a final check before the eunuch chief gave work assignments to the successful candidates.

Generally speaking the eunuchs came from the following three backgrounds: first, the sons of impoverished families, who became eunuchs only for a living; second, the children who had been abducted by criminals; third, criminal offenders who wanted to avoid punishment by being castrated. Therefore, the eunuchs from the above-mentioned backgrounds were mostly teen-age boys. In the Qing dynasty there were two families in Beijing whose profession was castrating young boys to be sent to the Imperial Palace as eunuchs. One was Bi family living in Nanchangjie Street, and the other was Liu family living near Di'anmen. Both Mr. Bi and Mr. Liu were officials of the 7th rank. They sent 40 eunuchs into the palace every three months in the year. The recruitment procedures were as follows: First, the boys who would become eunuchs applied to either of the two families, then they would be interviewed by Mr. Liu or Mr. Bi, who not only evaluated the applicants' appearance, speech and wisdom, but also examined their genital organs. The qualified would be kept in, waiting for the operation. Soon came the day when they were tied to the operation table just like an animal to be butchered. the scalpel was just put in a fire for a few minutes, and the genital organs were removed without any anaesthetization. This would naturally cause terrible pain and severe suffering on these poor boys. After the operation, a tube had to be inserted into the urethra in case it was sealed up in the course of granulation. Had this occurred, a second operation would be necessary. Therefore, after the testes were removed, it was not advisable to let the cut scar over quickly. Healing should generally take about 100 days. However, the dressings had to be changed frequently, which were a paper-thin mixture of white wax, sesame oil and powder of Chinese prickly ash. The boy who had been operated on had to lie on his back constantly. After four months, if he had recovered, the boy would be sent into the palace. But before entering, they had to stay for a few days in a temporary lodging arranged by the Punishment Department under the General Administration of the Royal House. The officials of the department would register their names and age, and then submit the list to the Administration for approval.

After they came into the palace, the young eunuchs began learning court etiquette. For example, before he answered his master's questions or extended his daily greetings to him or her, the eunuch had to kneel down, left knee first and right knee second, with his hat put on his right side. When he expressed his thanks to his master for his or her kindness or gifts, the eunuch had to kneel down three times and kowtow nine times. Sometimes, in order to show his extreme gratitude to his master, he had to bang his head on the floor. Besides this, the eunuch had to genuflect to his supervisor.

Marriage of the Eunuchs

From the Han dynasty to the Qing dynasty there had been records of eunuchs' marriage. In the Tang dynasty, Gao Lishi was the first eunuch in history to marry by permission of the emperor. In the dynasties that followed, it was quite common for the eunuchs to marry palace maids. After getting married, the eunuch and the palace-maid shared their properties and were treated as husband and wife.

In the Ming dynasty, Emperor Tian Qi personally made the decision that Lady Ke, his wet nurse, marry Wei Zhongxian, his favourite eunuch. Lady Ke became the wet nurse of the emperor at the age of 18. She first had a love affair with Wei Chao, a powerful eunuch, who later on brought Wei Zhongxian into the palace. Sharing the same family name, the two eunuchs soon became sworn brothers. But Wei Zhongxian was sly and crafty. He seduced Lady Ke and turned her into his own mistress. One day in the summer of 1621, in the West Warm Chamber of the Palace of Heavenly Purity, Wei Zhongxian and Wei Chao had a battle over who should possess Lady Ke. Their quarreling woke up Emperor Tian Qi, who came downstairs and ordered that the two men and the woman be brought before him. Having sympathy for Lady Ke, the emperor asked her, "Just tell me who you love, and I'll give the ruling." She responded by talking about Wei Chao with detestation. The next day Wei Zhongxian, with a false edict, forced Wei Chao to take sick-leave and eventually eliminated him. From then on Wei Zhongxian and Lady Ke lived together just like a married couple. Emperor Xuan De of the same dynasty once granted Chen Wu, his favourite eunuch, two palace maids as his wives.

Xiao Dezhang, a eunuch in late Qing dynasty, was brought into the palace when Ci Xi was in power. He once served Emperor Guang Xu and Empress Long Yu. After the downfall of the Qing dynasty, he moved to Tianjin and settled in the British Concession. He married a girl named Zhang Xiaoxian. It was said that he even had a few concubines. Usually the married eunuchs would not permit their wives to talk to male adults or go outside. Some eunuchs relied on their young pretty wives to find favour with the emperor. For example, in the late Qing dynasty, Gu Yuxiu, a eunuch in the Imperial Kitchen, with the help of his young wife, received a promotion to superintendent.

The Number of Eunuchs

The number of eunuchs varied from dynasty to dynasty. In the Ming dynasty, the eunuchs in the Imperial Palace were as many as 100,000. In the Qing dynasty, Emperor Kang Xi reduced the number of eunuchs from 100,000 to 9,000 and sent 7,000 of them to the border areas. Under the reign of Emperor Qian Long, the number of the eunuchs working in 127 sections was cut down to 2,866. As the Qing dynasty was declining, the number kept decreasing. During the reign of the last emperor, there were only 48 sections with 1,517 eunuchs.

In the Qing dynasty it was stipulated that two superintendent eunuchs with the sixth official rank, four supervising eunuchs with the eighth official rank and 46 eunuchs be employed in the palace of the empress dowager; one supervising eunuch with the 8th official rank and 10 eunuchs be employed for each concubine of the deceased emperor; one chief eunuch with the 7th official rank and 12 eunuchs be employed in the palace of the empress; 10 eunuchs be employed for each of the imperial concubines of the first, second and third rank; eight eunuchs for the fourth rank, four eunuchs for the 5th rank, three eunuchs for the 6th rank and one eunuch for the 7th rank.

A new-born prince was served by four eunuchs under the supervision of one chief eunuch with the 8th official rank. Three more eunuchs were added to his service when the prince was two years old. Another three were brought in when he was six years old. Then five more eunuchs were employed when he reached the age of 12. The number of eunuchs at his service totalled 28 after he got married.

A new-born princess was served by four eunuchs under the supervision of one chief eunuch (with no official rank). Two more eunuchs were added to her service when she was two years old. The princess took these eunuchs along with her when she got married. A grandson of the emperor was served by four eunuchs and one supervising eunuch (with no official rank). Two more eunuchs were added to his service at the age of two, and another two eunuchs were brought in at the age of six. Four more eunuchs were employed at the age of 12 and three more were assigned to him when he got married. A great grandson was served by two eunuchs and one supervising eunuch (with no official rank) when he was born, and two more eunuchs were added to his service after he got married.

Besides serving the emperor and his wives, the eunuchs also worked for his relatives. The number of eunuchs assigned varied according to the official position of the relative. In 1684 Emperor Kang Xi set a quota on the number of eunuchs employed by the brothers of the emperor and the other high-ranking officials. The quota goes as follows:
25 for the brothers of the emperor
20 for the provincial governors of royal descent
15 for the sons of the emperor's close relatives
10 for the daughters of the emperor's close relatives
2 for the officials of the first rank
1 for the officials of the second rank
The officials under the second rank were not allowed to employ any eunuchs.

Ranks of the Eunuchs

In 1722 Emperor Kang Xi promoted one chief eunuch and three supervising eunuchs to the 5th official rank, and two other eunuchs to the 6th official rank. This was how the eunuchs began to hold official ranks. In the first year of Yong Zheng's reign, the emperor decided that the Chief of Jinshifang (the Department in charge of eunuch affairs) should take the fourth offcial rank; the deputy Chief the sixth official rank; the supervising eunuch serving the emperor the seventh official rank; the supervising eunuchs working in various palaces the eighth official rank.

During the reign of Guang Xu in the Qing dynasty, Li Lianying, the most powerful eunuch then, was promoted to the second official rank by Empress Dowager Ci Xi, who also bestowed on him the official hat and yellow jackets with dragon design. It was a very special case in history. The deposed emperor Pu Yi once promoted Zhang Qianhe, the eunuch chief, Ruan Jinshou, the deputy chief, and Zhang De'an, the superintendent, to the second official rank.

The eunuchs who had official ranks all wore official hats with buttons of precious stones on top, and court dresses with embroidered insignias over the breast. The senior eunuchs without official ranks wore purple, silk robes with breast insignia of dragon design. The rank-and-file eunuchs wore blue cloth robes or purple cloth robes with no insignia.

The Later Life of the Aged Eunuchs and Their Cemetery

In the Qing dynasty the eunuchs usually came from Hebei province, Shangong province or Mongolia. They were thrown out of the palace after they became too old to work. As a rule, these aged eunuchs would settle down in temples. Therefore, when they were still young, the eunuchs began to save money, invest in real estate, contribute to the construction of temples and became disciples of Buddhist monks, so that they could find a place to spend their remaining years after they left the palace. In Beijing there were altogether 26 temples built in the Ming and Qing times respectively. The eunuchs who lived in temples derived a good income from real estates or land rent. Besides they were also engaged in farm business, such as growing grain, vegetables or fruits. Their farms were sometimes as large as several thousand mu each (6 mu to an acre), and their orchards were each more than ten thousand mu in area.

In 1735 the Qing court allotted 463 mu of farmland in the western suburbs to build a large cemetery for the eunuchs.

Emperor Yong Zheng granted 10,000 taels of silver to cover the cost of its construction. Apart from that, the statistics indicated that there were 3,336 eunuchs' tombs located in 16 temples or monasteries, where they spent their remaining years.

The Palace Maids

Chinese emperors practised polygamy through centuries. The employment of large number of palace maids dated back to thousands of years ago. According to historical records, in the Zhou dynasty (1122-249 B.C.) the emperor had three empresses and 117 concubines. In the Western Han period (206 B.C.-7 A.D.) the concubines in the inner palace were as many as several thousand. In the Tang dynasty during the reign of Emperor Xuan Zong there were 120 concubines, including Lady Yang, the emperor's favourite concubine. Superficially this meant a restoration of the imperial marriage system of the Zhou Dynasty. However, in the summer palaces in Luoyang and other cities, the number of concubines and palace maids amounted to 40,000. Bai Juyi, one of the best-known poet of the Tang dynasty, described their life with the following lines: "In the Inner Palace dwelt three thousand palace maids with heavy make-up, but few showed no trace of tears on their faces."

. The number of palace maids varied with the dynasties. In the Ming dynasty there were 9,000 of them in the Forbidden City alone. The food supply could not meet the needs of such a large number of female servants. everyday some of the poor girls would die of starvation. Emperor Jia Jing got the biggest number of palace maids in the Ming dynasty. Once he gave the following directive to the cabinet:

"My palace is short of servants. Though there are nearly 1,000 palace maids here, they are not enough to meet the needs of the imperial consorts since many of them are either too old or too weak from chronic diseases. The two princes and four princesses will leave the palace when they grow up. The princes will each take away over 30 palace maids and the princesses will each take away over 20. This is the tradition. Since training palace maids usually takes several years, their recruitment has to be started right away."

Immediately after that, Fei Cain, the Minister of Rites, decided to select palace maids from among the girls who lived in the suburbs of Beijing, or came from Hunan and Guangdong provinces. Such selection was made in the 26th, 31st, 34th and 43rd years of Jia Jing's reign. 1,080 girls aged 11 to 14 were chosen and brought into the palace, making the total number of palace maids more than 2,000.

Emperor Jia Jing employed a large number of palace maids not only for sexual pleasure, but also for his religious belief. In his late years he became a fanatic believer of Taoism. In order to live an eternal life, the emperor, on the advice of some Taoist priests, took the elixir, which was made from the first menstrual blood of the young girls. And this practice led to the attempted assasination that took place on November 27, 1542. Fourteen palace maids could not bear such insult, so they worked together in an attempt to strangle the emperor to death. But these girls were so panic-stricken that they tied

a Gordian knot by mistake and the emperor was quickly rescued. All the girls were immediately arrested and finally decapitated before the public.

A palace maid could be promoted to be an imperial concubine if the emperor had a liking for her. Lady Wan, a concubine of Emperor Zhu Jianshen of the Ming dynasty, was a typical example. She was brought into the palace to keep the empress dowager company. When she had grown up, she became the house-maid serving Zhu Jianshen, the crown prince then. On February 27, 1464, the 18-year-old Zhu Jianshen was enthroned. Although she was already 35 years old, Lady Wan still looked chubby and charming. As she was very smart and good at catering to the emperor's every wish, she managed to win his favour continuously, and was promoted concubine of the second rank. Later on Emperor Zhu happened to see another pretty girl-attendant, Lady Ji, in the stack-room of the Royal Library. He liked her very much and brought her to his bed-chamber. After she became pregnant, Lady Ji was promoted concubine of the third rank. Emperor Zhu Yijun of the same dynasty went to see his mother one day, and happened to see Miss Wang, a palace maid, taking a bath. He slept with her and she became pregnant soon after. So Miss Wang was subsequently promoted concubine of the third rank. Although these three palace maids were lucky enough to be promoted imperial concubine, they all ended up in tragedy. Lady Ji died a sudden death, and Lady Wan died of sorrow.

When they fell ill, the palace maids

were not treated inside the Forbidden City. They were usually taken to Anletang (the Happy Retreat), a place where the sick and old palace maids stayed. The guilty palace maids also stayed there before being sent to work at the Royal Laundry House. Anletang used to be located somewhere near Beihai (North Sea) with more than 20 staff members.

In terms of selecting palace maids, the Qing emperors built up a very strict system. The girls who were chosen to serve in the palace were divided into two ranks: Xiunü (the upper rank) and Gongnü (the lower rank). Xiunü were daughters of officials of the Eight Banners, and enjoyed superior status. They were usually assigned to serve the emperor and the empress, or became the candidates when the sons and grandsons of the emperor or the emperor's brothers and their sons were to choose their wives. Although the ceremony of picking wives varied in elaboration, the procedures were basically the same. Gongnü worked only as servants in the palace. They were daughters of the rank-and-file members of the three banners under the Royal Household Department. Though they came from humble families, Gonnü still had the chance to be promoted to imperial concubines.

According to historical records, every three years the commander of each banner had to submit a list of all the girls in that banner who were turning 13 years old, to the Ministry of Interior before the selection for Xiunü began. Once every year the Royal Household Department would select gongnü in the lst month of the Lunar calendar from among the girls within the three banners under its jurisdiction. The age limit was between 13 and 16. Those who were older than 16 had to wait for their turn until all the girls of the right age had gone through the selection process. Those who were unable to turn up at the time of selection because of sickness were allowed to show up at the next selection.

The palace maids were usually from the following families:

1. Those of officials, soldiers or the unemployed in the Eight Banners.

2. The civil and the military officials of the Royal Household Department who were stationed outside the capital, still had to send their daughters to Beijing for the selection. The girls suffered a great deal during the long journey to the capital and back. Since the 8th year of Qian Long's reign, these girls were exempted from travelling over long distance to the capital for the selection. Instead, a name-list of all the 12-year-old girls was made and then submitted to the eunuch-in-chief for the selection.

3. In the 45th year of Qian Long's reign, the officials of the third rank or higher, who were stationed at Miyun, Liangxiang and Shunyi, were ordered to send their daughters for the selection.

4. In the 11th year of Jia Qing's reign, the adjutants and majors or higher in the Royal Army were ordered to send their daughters for the selection.

5. In the 18th year of Jia Qing's reign, the captains or higher of the Mongol Self-Defense Army in Manchuria were ordered to send their daughters for the

selection.

The following families were excluded from sending their daughters for the selection:

1. Under the reign of Kang Xi, the girls of the close relatives of the royal family, or whose mothers came from the royal family, were immune from the selection.

2. The daughters of the brothers or sisters of the imperial concubines were not entitled to the selection.

3. The daughters of petty clerks were not supposed to go for the selection.

4. The daughters of the emperor's wet-nurse were not included in this selection.

5. The daughters of the minorities in the three banners under the Royal Household Department were barred from the selection.

6. The girls of the Han nationality, but adopted by the Manchus, had no right to take part in the selection.

Interview of Palace Maid Candidates

The selection of Gongnü took place every year. The Royal Household Department would set a date for the interview three months in advance. The number of girls to be interviewed averaged about 80 each time. Everyday the girls from two banners would be examined. The day before the selection, the commanders and other important officials of each banner would arrange the order of the carts

which were to take the girls to the Imperial Palace. They first divided the carts into three groups: the Manchu first, the Mongol second and the Han the last. In each group the order of the carts was determined by the age of the girl candidates. All these carts were moving on in file, one girl in each cart. two lanterns with markings hung on both sides of the cart. The procession set out at dusk, and passed Dianmen City Gate when night fell. Finally the carts would arrive at the north gate of the Forbidden City (the Gate of Divine Prowess). When the gate was opened, the girls got off their carts one after another and walked into the palace. Then all the carts moved into the palace through the north gate and left there through the East Flowery Gate. Afterwards they would make a round-about trip, turning south first, then west, and then back to the north of the city. From Dianmen City Gate they rolled on and eventually stopped before the north gate of the Imperial Palace again, waiting for these girls. By that time it was about noon the next day. Having been interviewed the girls would get on the carts and leave for home. Although there were as many as over a thousand carts, the selection process went on smoothly in a perfect order. Each girl had to rent her own cart and was paid in advance one tael of silver for that purpose.

Having entered the Gate of Divine Prowess, the girls stood in line, waiting outside Shunzhenmen Gate. The interview was supervised by the officials from the Ministry of Interior. When the interview began, eunuchs would usher in five girls each time according to the prearranged namelist. The girls stood in a row in front of the Gate of Earthly Tranquility or the Gate of Prolonged Elegance. Each girl wore a blue cotton gown, which had been given them free of charge, with a white wooden tablet hanging from the first button on the right. The tablet was six inches long and two inches wide, and on it were written the girl's name and her father's name and his official position. Those who were chosen at the first interview would have their tablets kept by the examining officials, and they had to come again for the second interview. If the officials didn't keep the girl's tablet, it meant she had been rejected.

Having been admitted into the palace, the girls began to learn not only court etiquette, but also reading and writing. They had to take a test after one year of training. The top ones would be assigned to serve the empress or the imperial concubines. The rest of them would be given other jobs, such as taking care of clothes or jewellery. The number of palace maids serving in each palace varied with the position of the lady living in that palace. During the reign of Emperor Kang Xi, it was stipulated:

12 palace maids for the empress dowager

10 palace maids for the empress

8 palace maids for the imperial concubine of the lst rank

8 palace maids for the imperial concubine of the second rank

6 palace maids for the imperial concubine of the third rank

6 palace maids for the imperial con-

cubine of the 4th rank

4 palace maids for the imperial concubine of the 5th rank

3 palace maids for the imperial concubine of the 6th rank

1 palace maids for the imperial concubine of the 7th rank

Remuneration for the palace maids:

Each palace maid received, as their annual pay, 6 taels of silver, a length of satin, 3 rolls of silk, a length of gauze, one roll of silk thread, and 3 catties of cotton. Everyday each palace-maid was provided with one catty of pork, 12 taels of fresh vegetables, 0.75 pint of rice, and 0.3 tael of salt.

Remuneration for the palace maids who served in the palaces of the princes and the imperial concubines:

Each palace maid received, as their annual pay, 5 taels of silver, 2 rolls of silk, 2 catties of cotton. Everyday each was provided with one catty of pork, 0.75 pint of rice, 0.3 tael of salt and 12 taels of fresh vegetables.

Remuneration for the palace maids who worked in other palaces:

Each palace maid received, as their annual pay, 5 taels of silver, one roll of silk, four rolls of cloth, 2 catties of cotton. Everyday each was provided with half catty of pork, 0.75 pint of rice, 0.3 tael of salt and 12 taels of fresh vegetables.

The Duration of Service in the Palace and the Final Reward

A palace maid entered the palace at the age of 13 and usually left the palace after having worked for more than ten years. Under the reign of Emperor Kang Xi it was stipulated that the palace maids could not leave the palace until the age of 30. Under the reign of Emperor Yong Zheng, the palace maids were allowed to leave the palace for good at the age of 25, and then their parents could arrange their marriage.

At the end of their service the palace maids who served the empress dowager, the empress and the imperial concubines of the lst, second, third and 4th rank would get rewards from their masters. The palace maids who served the imperial concubines of the fifth rank or under for longer than 15 years would receive 30 taels of silver as reward from the court. Those who served in the palace less than 15 years would receive 20 taels, and less than 10 years, 10 taels. The palace maids who were ejected from the palace for wrong-doings got no reward.

The Rules of Conduct for Palace Maids

1. The former palace maids who have left the palace are not allowed to come into the palace again, nor can they send

somebody to extend their greetings to their old masters.

2. Palace maids are not allowed to take eunuchs as their relatives, nor can they talk to them, laugh or make noise with them unless they get the permission to do so from their masters.

3. The eunuchs in charge of the palaces should make way for palace maids if they run into them on their way.

4. In case they address the eunuchs as uncles or brothers, the palace maids of the six palaces will be flogged and ejected from the palace, and their relatives will be exiled to Xinjiang.

5. When a palace maid is ordered to leave the palace by her master because of sickness, clumsiness or bad conduct, the chief eunuch must verify the case and report to the emperor for approval before the palace maid in question is allowed to leave.

For several thousand years this tragic system of palace maids had prevailed through the history. These girls lost contact with their families as soon as they entered the palace. They had to serve in the palace for more than ten years before they were allowed to go home and get married. By that time their youth had been gone. A small number of them were lucky enough to become imperial concubines, but most of them worked very hard, waiting on the empress and the concubines. They got up early and went to bed late in the night, endured untold hardships and often fell ill because of heavy work. Some of them could not bear the sufferings and tried to run away from the palace. some girls pretended to be stupid so that they might find excuse to leave the palace. Some took each other as husband and wife; some even married the eunuchs. The palace maids should have disappeared together with the downfall of the last feudal dynasty. However, owing to the existence of the small court headed by the last emperor, the system of palace maids lasted for another 13 years. In September 1923 due to financial difficulties and the ever-growing pressure from the society, the small court decided to dismiss a large number of palace maids. Each of them was given 100 silver dollars and left the palace to make their own living. The history of palace maids came to an end at last.

Cultural Relics
Attached to
the Palace

Huabao of Tian'anmen

Before and behind the magnificent Tian'anmen (Gate of Heavenly Peace) stand two pairs of sculpted white marble columns called huabiao. Each column measures 9.57 meters in height and weighs over 10,000 kilograms. The body of the column is elegantly sculptured with beautiful cloud designs and a huge dragon entwining it. On the top is a chenglupan (plate for collecting dew), on which squats a stone mythical animal. At the bottom is an octagonal marble base surrounded by stone balustrades. They look both solemn and splendid against the blue sky.

The history of huabiao dates back to the times of Shun, a legendary monarch some 4,000 years ago. According to *Huainanzi*, a book written by Liu Xiang of the Han dynasty, King Shun put up feibangmu (wooden post for writing comments on wrong doings) at major crossroads, so that people could put down their criticisms on them. By so doing the monarch meant to show his willingness to accept the views of the common people. Feibangmu gradually evolved into huabiao in later years.

In the Zhou dynasty huabiao were also used as road signs. In the Han dynasty huabiao were erected as ornamental pillars in front of bridges, city walls, palaces and tombs. Huabiao were usually made of wood until the Han dynasty when they were mostly made of stone. Eventually huabiao became architectural ornaments of the imperial palaces after they had gained artistic perfection.

The squatting mythical animal at the top of each huabiao in front of Tian'anmen is called "hou". It faces south, gazing into the distance. The legend says that hou kept an eye on the emperor while he was on an inspection tour. It often persuaded the emperor not to spend too much time travelling from place to place, and also reminded him to return to the capital to attend to state affairs. Therefore, it was commonly known as wangjungui (expecting the emperor's return). The hou on each of the huabiao behind Tian'anmen faces north, watching the emperor in the Forbidden City. The legend goes that it often advised the emperor against indulging himself in merry-making with his empress and concubines, and admonished him to leave the palace and find out about the people's sufferings. Therefore, it was commonly known as wangjunchu (awaiting the emperor's come out).

Bronze Lions

Bronze lions or gilded bronze lions were placed in front of the palace gates, not only to show off the luxury of the royal court, but also to manifest the dignity of the emperor.

Inside the Forbidden City there are seven pairs of bronze lions cast respectively in the Ming and Qing dynasties. For each pair, the one on the west side is female with a baby lion under its left paw; the one on the east is male with an embroidered ball under its right paw. Both lions are looking at the central passageway. These seven pairs of bronze lions are all beautifully cast and life-like. The pair of bronze lions in front of the Gate of Supreme Harmony is not only the largest in size, but also excellent in workmanship. The other six pairs are all gilded bronze lions.

Phoenix

The phoenix in Chinese legend is a divine bird. The *Annotations on Characters* explains: "The phoenix is a divine bird. According to Tian Lao its first half looks like that of a swan goose and its latter half looks like that of a Chinese unicorn. It has a snake's neck, fish's tail, stork's forehead, mandarin duck's cheeks, tiger's back, swallow's chin and chicken's beak. Its plume has all the five colors. It is a native of a gentlemen's state in the East."

In primitive society some tribes worshipped phoenix as their totem. Oracle inscriptions on bones or tortoise shells of the Shang dynasty describe the bird as a messenger of Heavenly King. Many bronze objects bear patterns of phoenix. Many ancient books mention it. The classic of *Mountains and Rivers* says: "At the tomb of Emperor Xuanyuan the luan (a mythical bird) sings and pheonix dances." Another ancient book *Huan Nan Zi* says: "During the time of the two emperors (Fu Xi and Shen Nong) the phoenix appeared at the courtyard; during the time of the three kings (Yao, Shun and

Yu) the phoenix appeared at the gate. " "Lisao" (The Lament) a poem by great patriot Qu Yuan of the Warring States period, writes: "I order the phoenix to fly high. "

All this shows that in ancient China the phoenix was regarded as a beautiful, auspicious bird. In 1949 some silk paintings were unearthed from tombs of the Warring States period at Changsha. One depicts a fight between a phoenix and an uggly monkey. The phoenix at an advantageous point defeats the evil monkey. Legend has it that when the phoenix appeared the world would be at peace. When it traveled all the birds followed. In imperial times the phoenix was the symbol of the empress.

Bronze Tortoise and Bronze Crane

The bronze tortoises and bronze cranes are symbols of long life. They are placed on the marble terraces of the Hall of Supreme Harmony and the Hall of Imperial Supremacy. Each of them has a movable lid at its back, and a hollow belly extending to the mouth. In the old days during a grand ceremony, sandalwood, dried pine and cypress branchs were burnt inside the bodies of these bronze tortoises and cranes, which poured forth coiling smoke around the hall so as to create a mysterious and solemn atmosphere for the ceremony.

Both the cranes and the tortoises before the Hall of Imperial Supremacy were

cast in 1773. The crane measures 5.6 feet high and weighs 1,092 kilograms. The casting of the two cranes cost 2,280 mandays of labor and 412 taels of silver. The tortoise measures 2.6 feet high and weighs 1,988 kilograms. The casting of the two tortoises cost 4,193 mandays of labor and 645 taels of silver.

Xie Zhi

At the Tianyimen Gate in the Imperial Garden squat two gilded bronze xie zhi, a kind of divine animals in the ancient Chinese mythology. It has a dragon's head and claws, a lion's tail and a single horn. According to historical books, xie zhi was the animal that could judge what was right and what was wrong, and was once involved in trying a case. In the Han, Tang and Song dynasties, the censors wore hats shaped like xie zhi. In the Ming and Qing dynasties, the censors wore official uniforms embroidered with the images of xie zhi. Therefore, xie zhi had become a symbol of justice in ancient China. So this pair of xie zhi placed at Tianyimen Gate was intended to show that the emperor was an enlightened monarch since he resorted to xie zhi's help to detect wicked officials.

Gilded Bronze Qi Lin

In front of the Gate of Motherly Tranquility is a pair of gilded bronze qi lin, an imaginary animal in the ancient

mythology. It looks like a deer, but with a dragon's head, a lion's body, ox's hooves and fish's scales. Legend says that qi lin is an intelligent animal besides dragon, phoenix and tortoise, so its deified image can be widely seen in the Chinese folk arts just like those of dragons and phoenixes.

Gilded Bronze Elephants

A pair of gilded bronze elephants can be seen kneeling at Chengguangmen Gate in the Imperial Garden. The decorations on them indicate that they were modelled after the elephants kept in the Imperial Palace. Elephant-raising in the palaces dates back to a long time. As early as in the Zhou dynasty elephants were used to guide the royal procession. In the dynasties that followed, elephants were tamed either for riding or pulling the emperor's carriage. In the Ming and Qing dynasties there were elephant training grounds. The royal procession escorting the Qing emperor was always headed by elephants. During a grand ceremony, five elephants stood before the Meridian Gate, guarding the entrance. Everyday in the early morning, four elephants stood on duty in front of of the Gate of Heavenly Peace.

The gilded bronze elephants at Chengguangmen Gate also symbolize peace and bumper harvest.

Stone Pavilion and Stone Casket

To the left of the Gate of Supreme Harmony is a little stone pavilion with a grain measure inside. To the right is a stone casket made of marble. A coiling dragon is engraved on the lid. Grain used to be put inside the casket to betoken good harvest.

Sundial

A sundial is a device for showing the time of day from the shadow cast by an upright pin on a dial. The application of sundials can be traced back to the Zhou dynasty (1122-249 B. C). In the Qin and Han dynasties they were already used widely in the country.

A sundial has an iron pin in the centre of the stone dial, with its upper end pointing to the north pole and its lower end to the south pole. The stone dial is marked with 24 lines (15 degrees between two lines). Twelve Chinese characters were carved on both sides of the stone dial, which stand for the twelve hours of the duodecimal cycle. Time is shown when the shadow of the pin falls on the character. In spring and summer people looked at the upper side of the dial, whereas in autumn and winter at the lower side.

The sundial to the east of the Hall of Supreme Harmony is placed on a 2. 7-meter-high marble support. The stone dial is 725 mm in diameter and 85 mm in thickness. The iron pin with sharpened ends is 342 mm long on each side. The stone dial and its flat base form an angle of 50 degrees. Under the base four square columns stand on a marble bottom with stone steps on the north and south sides.

Moondial

The only moondial in the Forbbiden City is placed in front of the Palace of Earthly Tranquility. A magnetic pin is used to indicate the direction. Time is measured by the shade of moonlight. A history note records the use of a moondial:

"The moondial is made of copper and has two disks of a diameter of five inches. The lower disk indicates 12 time periods; the upper disk is divided into 360 degrees and 30 days. "

Jia Liang
(Grain Measure)

Jia liang is the grain measure used in ancient China. On each of the marble terraces before the Hall of Supreme Harmony, the Palace of Heavenly Purity and the Hall of Imperial Supremacy, a jia liang, made of bronze and then gilded, was placed inside a small marble pavilion as the standard measure for the whole country.

The square jia liang displayed before the Hall of Supreme Harmony was modelled after those made in the Tang dynasty (618-906 A. D.). The round jia liang put in front of the Palace of Heavenly Purity was modelled after those made under the reign of Wang Mang in the Xing dynasty (8-23 A. D.). Both of those two grain measures were cast in 1744 in the reign of Qian Long as a symbol of national unification.

Tripod Incense Burners

On the marble terraces of the Hall of Supreme Harmony stand 18 bronze tripod incense burners cast in the Ming dynasty. During grand ceremonies incense was burnt in them so as to add solemnity to the atmosphere. Four gilded bronze tripod incense burners cast in the reign of Qian Long were placed respectively before the Palace of Heavenly purity and the Hall of Imperial Supremacy. Two bronze tripod incense burners with the design of animal faces, cast in the reign of Jia Qing, were placed in front of the Hall of Cultivating the Mind and the Palace of Assisting the Empress. Eight small tripod incense burners were placed before the Hall of Manifesting Harmony, a part of Empress Dowager Ci Xi's residence. Each of them is 80 cm in height and stands on a 134-cm high marble base, so they are the smallest tripod incense burners in the palace. The four-meter-high tripod incense burner standing in front of Tianyimen Gate in the Imperial Garden is the largest in this palace and superb in craftsmanship. Incense was burnt in it when the emperor went to worship the god in the Hall of Imperial Peace.

Jiangshan Pavilion and Sheji Pavilion

There is a gilded pavilion on each side of the marble terrace before the Palace of Heavenly Purity. The one on the east is called Jiangshan Pavilion, which is square in shape with four door slabs on each side. Its double eaves, round on top and square underneath, symbolize the ancient belief that the earth was square and the heaven was round. The gilded pavilion sits on a three-tier stone base, 350 cm high and 550 cm square, carved with sea wave and cliff designs. The whole structure of the pavilion, which is a symbol of territorial integrity, is in perfect harmony with the magnificent Palace of Heavenly Purity.

The one on the west of the marble terrace is Sheji Pavilion. Sheji stands for the God of Land and Grain. Therefore, the pavilion served as a symbol of bumper harvest.

Bronze Road Lamps

Bronze road lamps are seen in front of the Gate of Heavenly Purity and around the Six Eastern and Western Palaces. Each lamp is 245 cm high including the marble base. The square lamp shade is shaped like a pavilion with double eaves and paned on four sides. In the Ming dynasty, the road lamps had only wired shades without glass. Everyday before night fell, eunuchs would light these lamps. In the late Ming times, Wei Zhongxian, the eunuch chief, gave order that all the road lamps be taken away so that he and his henchmen could carry out secret activities at night. In the Qing dynasty the wired lamp shades were replaced by glass lamp shades.

Nine-Dragon Screen

It is located near the Outer Eastern Palaces just off Xiqing Gate. The screen faces the north and served as the screen wall of the Gate of Imperial Supremacy. Erected in 1771 with 270 glazed multicolored tiles, this wall-like screen is 3.5 meters high and 29.4 meters wide with an exquisitely-carved stone base. In the centre of the screen is a yellow dragon flanked on two sides by eight dragons in various postures. From a distance visitors can see the nine dragons romping in the sea against a background of waves, cliffs and clouds.

Besides this nine-dragon screen there is another one in Beihai Park, which was put up in 1756 and has nine dragons on both sides. The third nine-dragon screen is situated in Datong, Shanxi province. It was built in 1392 as the screen wall for the mansion of Prince Zhu, the 13th son of Zhu Yuanzhang, the founder of the Ming dynasty.

Arrow Heads Embedded in Longzongmen Gate

Longzongmen is the west gate of the Inner Court. Today visitors still can see arrow heads sticking out at the top of it. They were left there during a fierce fight between the palace security forces and the peasant insurgents commanded by the Society of Nature's Law, who broke into the Forbidden City in 1813. The Society of Nature's Law, also called the Society of Eight Diagrams, was a branch organization of the Society of White Lotus. Its members were mostly peasants and craftsmen from Shandong, Hebei, Henan and Shanxi provinces, who were organized into many secret units under the cloak of religion. A plan to launch an attack on the Imperial Palace was formulated by Lin Qing, head of the society, Hebei Branch. He once lived in the western part of Beijing and often went to the quail market near Xi'anmen City Gate. He found out that some court eunuchs also frequented the place. So he disguised himself as a quail dealer. In time he converted some eunuchs to the society and made them his planted agents.

On October 8, 1813 the peasant insurgents led by Lin Qing entered the city in secret through Xuanwumen City Gate, because the security inspection was then slackened after the emperor had left the capital to go hunting at Rehe. They were disguised as pedlars and coolies with white towels around their heads as the signal. At noon, over 100 peasant insurgents, with the help of seven eunuchs, stormed the palace through East Flowery and West Flowery Gates. Just at the time when the peasants were rushing into the palace through East Flowery Gate under the guidance of Liu Jing, a court eunuch, a skirmish broke out between the peasants and some workers who were carting coal into the palace. When they discovered the peasants with hidden weapons, the guards quickly closed the gate, leaving many peasants outside. Those who had managed to come in fought their way to Jingyunmen, the east gate of the Inner Court. On the eave of the gate a few arrow heads left from the battle can still be seen today. The other team of peasant insurgents led by Gao Guangfu, another eunuch, entered the West Flowery Gate successfully, and occupied a few buildings. When they were approaching the emperor's residence—the Hall of Cultivating the Mind, a bloody battle was fought against the imperial guards near Longzongmen Gate. The arrow heads embedded in the nameplate, the gatepost and the eave were all left from the fighting. Soon the Qing court brought in reinforcements through the Gate of Divine Prowess. The surprise attack delivered by the peasant insurgents on the Imperial Palace was finally foiled owing to a great disparity in strength, and lack of ample preparations. Eight days later, Lin Qing was executed.

Although the peasant insurgents occupied a part of the Forbidden City for only one day, the attack dealt the Qing rulers hard blows. Emperor Jia Qing exclaimed, "This had never happened in the Han, Tang, Song and Ming dynasties!" The peasant uprising led by Lin Qing put the Qing rulers on tenterhooks and was recorded in the history of Beijing for their heroic and moving deeds.

Carved Stone Ramp

In the Forbidden City carved stone ramps of fine workmanship can be seen before or behind the main palace buildings. The one behind the Hall of Preserving Harmony is the largest piece of stone carving in the palace. It is 16.57 meters long, 3.07 meters wide, 1.7 meters thick, and weighs about 250 tons. The relief sculpture shows nine coiling dragons, which are vividly engraved and lifelike, playing amidst drifting clouds. It is widely regarded as a treasure of the ancient stone carving.

This piece of stone of enormous size was quarried in the Ming times at Shiwo village, Fangshan county, some 50 kilometers from Beijing. It was incredible to transport such a large piece of stone over long distance without modern equipment. According to historical records, 20,000 peasants were involved in this arduous project. Wells were sunk every half a kilometer in severe winter, and water was then brought up and poured over the road to make an ice-path. Pulled by a thousand horses and mules and pushed by ten thousand peasants, the huge stone slid slowly over the ice. This way it took 28 days to move the raw stone to Beijing and cost 110,000 taels of silver altogether.

In 1760 under the reign of Qian Long, this large stone ramp was recarved and the two smaller stone ramps above it were replaced costing 17,075 taels of silver.

Divine Pole

The Divine Pole is made of cedarwood and erected in front of the Palace of Earthly Tranquility. It is 416 cm long with a wooden bowl close to the top. Its stone base is 76 cm high and 51 cm square.

During the rite of worshipping heaven, a priest would detach the pole from its base, remove the old burnt paper and pig's neckbones from the bowl, and burn them in a copper basin. A red lacquered table was laid east of the pole with three silver plates on top. The plate to the west was filled with pig's neckbones and meat; the middle one with rice; the one to the east with gallbladder. Then the emperor and the empress, standing in the palace of Earthly Tranquility, bowed to the table and the pole. After that, the priest would spread the rice on the ground two times, puncture the neckbones with the sharpened top end of the pole, put the meat, the gall-bladder and the rice in the wooden bowl, and then put up the pole again. When the rite came to an end, the emperor and empress were offered meat in the west chamber of the palace.

Willow-Branch Stone

Willow-Branch Stone is in front of the Palace of Earthly Tranquility. A willow branch inserted into a hole in the stone with the other end tied to a shrine. It was prayed to protect safe birth of the emperor's children.

Several days before the ceremony, six court officials would go to Yingtai to supervise the cutting of branches from willow trees nine feet tall and three inches in diameter. The branches would be wrapped in yellow silk and kept in a clean place. On the day the branches would be placed under the eave of the Palace of Earthly Tranquility and decorated with a string of paper coins and tricolor silk pieces. The emperor and empress, kneeling at the sacrificial table, would spickle the willow branches with wine and place cakes on them. After the ceremony the willow branches would be burnt together with the paper coins.

Zhenfei's Well

In the northeast corner of the Forbidden City near Zhenshunmen Gate there is a well called Zhenfei's well. Zhenfei was Emperor Guang Xu's favourite concubine, but she was on bad terms with Empress Dowager Ci Xi who held power over both military and political affairs. After the 1898 Reform suffered a serious defeat, Ci Xi put Guang Xu under house arrest at Yingtai, Zhongnanhai, and Zhenfei was jailed in an out-of-the-way place in the palace.

In 1900 the anti-imperialist movement initiated by Yihetuan (Boxers' Uprising) broke out and the Allied Forces of Eight Powers invaded Beijing. On the 21st day of the 7th lunar month, Ci Xi coerced Guang Xu to run away with her to Xian. Shortly before her departure, she ordered eunuchs to bring Zhenfei out from her house of confinement (just behind the red wall next to the well) and forced her to jump into the well on the pretext that she would inevitably fall a victim to the invading foreign soldiers. Zhenfei protested and refused to do so. Then Cui Yugui, the assistant eunuch chief, pushed Zhenfei into the well at the order of Ci Xi. Zhenfei was only 25 years old when she was drowned in the well. According to Tang Guanqing and Chen Pingshun, both eunuchs, who witnessed the above tragic event, the stone ring on top of the well had already been removed, and quarreling between Ci Xi and Zhenfei could be heard from a distance. This means that the murder of Zhenfei had been preplanned.

Zhenfei's corpse was not fished out until the end of 1901. Guang Xu still cherished the memory of Zhenfei, so he promoted her posthumously to concubine of the first rank, and buried her at Enjizhuang outside Xizhimen City Gate. On November 16, 1913 the deposed Emperor Pu Yi gave the order that Zhenfei's coffin be reburied in the royal cemetery.

After the death of Ci Xi, Jinfei, Zhenfei's sister, set up a memorial hall to Zhenfei with a one-meter-high wooden tablet just opposite the well. Services were conducted there every fortnight.

Dragon

Dragon, just like the phoenix, was a totem of the premitive people in China. In the first Chinese dynasty Xia, the people all worshipped dragons as their totem. It was said that dragons could subdue monsters and ward off evil spirits. people in the ancient times thought dragons were capable of walking on land, swimming in water, flying in the sky, and invoking storms and floods. Therefore, the dragon was considered as one of the four intelligent animals (qi lin, phoenix, tortoise and dragon). In history all the feudal emperors used the image of dragons as their own symbol.

As a Chinese folktale goes, the dragon had nine sons which had different looks and interests. The first son was fond of music, so its image could often be seen on traditional musical instruments. The second son liked to kill, so the handles of the emperor's swords or daggers bore its image. The third son liked to take risks and it is seen on top of the upturned eaves of the palace buildings. The fourth son liked to utter a cry and its image was cast on the gold chimes played at grand ceremonies. The fifth son liked fire and smoke, so the feet of the tripod incense burners were cast into its image. The sixth son liked water and many water spouts were carved in the shape of its head. The seventh son liked solitude, therefore the gate knockers of the palace buildings were all modelled after its head. The eighth son liked to carry loads, such as stone tablets. The ninth son liked to swallow things and its head looks forward on the ridges of the palace buildings. In conclusion, we can say that the dragon's nine sons bear no resemblance to their father, and each has its own peculiar hobby.

Water Vats

The water vats scattered around in the Forbidden City were used for fire-prevention and also as a kind of decoration in the Ming and Qing dynasties.

In the Ming dynasty there were three types of water vats: iron, bronze and gilded bronze. The bronze vats had two or four handles with iron rings. In the Qing dynasty, most of the vats were bronze or gilded bronze ones. Each vat has handles in the shape of a beast's head. All these vats were filled up with water for fire-prevention. In cold winter all the vats were wrapped up in cotton-padded coverings with lids on the top. Besides, charcoal was kept burning inside the stone ring under the vat so as to prevent the water from freezing. The heating by charcoal fire continued until the Spring Festival passed. Whenever a grand ceremony was held, all these vats were covered with yellow cloth in order to add solemnity to the atmosphere.

Treasures on Display in the Palace

Ruyi

The history of ruyi can date back to the Han dynasty (206 B. C. -220 A. D.). However, in the early days it was meant for different purposes. The iron ruyi was carried as a weapon for self-protection. Buddhist monks held ruyi while preaching. But it was used most commonly as a back-scratcher. Ruyi is about three feet long with an S-shaped handle. Its top is made like a cloudlet. In later years ruyi gradually became an ornamental object or curio kept in palaces or aristocrats' mansions. In the residences of the emperor and empress, it was placed beside the royal seats or on the desks as a symbol of good luck. When the young emperor chose his wife, he would give a ruyi to the girl he liked best. Apart from that, ruyi was also a valuable gift. On such festive occasions as the emperor's coronation or birthday, the princes and ministers would present ruyi to the emperor, empress or imperial concubines as a gift. In the Qing dynasty, when Qian Long celebrated his 60th birthday, ministers offered him 60 gold ruyi, which were made with 1,361 ounces of gold. When Ci Xi celebrated her 60th birthday, ministers presented to her 81 ruyi (nine times nine). the emperor also bestowed ruyi on ministers in return for their loyalty.

In the Qing palaces a ruyi was about two feet long, and made of various valuable materials, such as gold, jade, jadeite, crystal, agate, coral, amber, etc. They are noted for the superb carving and flawless inlaid work.

Phoenix Crown

Phoenix was a symbol of good luck and beauty in the eyes of ancient people in China. It was thought to be the queen of birds and had been worhipped through all ages. In the Qin dynasty (221-207 B. C.) aristocratic ladies wore gold phoenix pins in the hair. In the Han dynasty the image of phoenix was used to decorate the crown of the empress.

There are two phoenix crowns on display in the Treasure Hall of the Palace Museum: one for the Ming empress with three dragons and two phoenixes, and the other one for the Qing empress. The crown with three dragons and two phoenixes was excavated from Ding Ling, one of the 13 Ming Tombs in the nortern suburb of Beijing, and used to be worn by Empress Xiao Duan, wife of Emperor Wan Li, on ceremonial occasions. It weighs two kilograms and is made of gold, kingfisher feathers, over 100 pieces of ruby and sapphire, and more than 5,000 pearls. The body of the crown is supported by a cone made of bamboo filaments. Three gold dragons sit on top of the clouds made of kingfisher feathers. The dragon in the forefront holds in its mouth a string of pearls and little pieces of ruby and sapphire. The other two dragons hold in their mouths long strings of 312 pearls and 15 gems. Twenty-four flowers, each is composed of one gem and 12 pearls, are inlaid in the round gold base. A close look may reveal more flowers in various sizes on the crown, which are made of of gems (as pistils), pearls (as petals), kingfisher feathers (as leaves). THe crown demonstrates not only the ingenious conception, but also amazing craftsmanship of the artisans.

In the Qing dynasty there were two types of crowns, one for summer wear and one for winter wear. The crown worn in winter was made of mink. The crown on display in th Treasure Hall was worn in summer and made of black flannel and trimmed with vermilion velvet. It has three gold phoenixes on top, one upon another, which was an important hallmark differentiating the rank of empress from the imperial concubines. Of all the existing phoenix crowns worn by the Qing empress and concubines, this one is the best preserved. It is decorated with ten gold phoenixes, a gold long-tailed pheasant, eight cat's eyes, 83 eastern pearls from northeast China and 436 other pearls.

Gold Goblet

In one of the Treasure Halls there is a gold goblet on show. It was used by emperors on every new Year's Day to drink tusu wine as a preventive against illness during the ceremony for writing the first characters of the new year.

Beginning from Yong Zheng, at 12 : 15 p. m. on the first day of the lunar New Year, the Qing emperor performed a ceremony for writing the first characters of the year. With the goldgoblet filled up with tusu wine on the desk, the emperor, brush in hand, would write some auspicious words, such as "World Peace" or "Everlasting Happiness and Longevity", which served as an omen of success in the new year.

This gold goblet was made in 1797 at the royal workshop. It is 12.5 cm high and 8 cm around the rim with three 5-cm stems. The two handles were cast in the shape of two dragons with two pearls on the top. The three stems were made in the shape of elephants' heads. The gold goblet itself weighs 20 ounces and is inlaid with 11 pearls, 4 aquamarines, 12 sapphires, 9 rubies. Four characters cut in relief on the goblet means territorial integrity and everlasting security. Therefore, the Qing emperors regarded this gold goblet as a family heirloom, which was to be handed down from generation to generation.

Jade Carving of Dayu Harnessing Flood

It is the largest piece of jade carving in China today, and now on display in one of the Treasure Halls in the Palace Museum. The jade stone, weighing two tons, is 224 cm high and sits on a 60-cm tall bronze base. This huge block of jade was quarried in Hetian, Xinjiang, northwest China. In that area, jade stone was quarried out either from rivers or in the mountains. Considering the non-existence of modern means of transportation, we can imagine how difficult it must have been to move a such gigantic block of jade stone all the way from Xinjiang to Beijing, covering a distance of thousands of kilometers. A cart of immense size was made

specially for the purpose. The cart was very wide and the axles ere as long as 35 feet. Pulled by over 100 horses and mules and pushed by 1,000 coolies, the cart loaded with the jade stone moved slowly forward. When a mountain stood in their way, they cut a passage through; when a river lay ahead, they built a bridge over it. In winter time, thery made an ice-path by pouring water over the road and then slid the stone on the ice. Altogether it took over three years to trans-port this enormous jade stone to Beijing. When the design for the carving was made at the order of the emperor, the raw jade was sent to Yangzhou. After the carving was finished there, it was shipped back to Beijing.

Chaozhu (beads worn in court)

Chaozhu was an ornament worn by Qing emperors, empresses, princes, dukes and high officials when they were in ceremonial dress. It was a variation of the ancient custom that all the aristocrats wore jade ornaments with their official garments. Therefore ordinary officials were not entitled to wear chaozhu.

At different places the emperor wore chaozhu made of different materials. At a grand ceremony in the palace he would wear one decorated with pearls; at the Temple of Heaven, one with lapis lazuli; at the Temple of Earth, one with topaz; at the Temple of Sun, one with coral; at the Temple of Moon, one with turquoise.

Although chaozhu may vary in materials, each string always consists of 108 round beads, signifving the belief that one year was composesd of 12 months, 24 solar terms and 72 periods of five days (hou). In between the beads four larger ones represented the four seasons. On the sides were attached three strings of smaller beads, two on the left and one on the right, each of 10 beads representing the first, second and last periods of 10 days in a month. The chaozhu made of eastern pearls from northeast China was for the exclusive use of emperors, empresses and empress dowagers.

Ivory Mat

Among the valuable objects preserved in the Qing palace is a rare treasure — an ivory mat made in the reign of Yong Zheng. It is 216 cm by 139 cm and woven of ivory filaments less than 0.3cm wide. The four edges of the mat were painted black with three lineal patterns. As it was extremely difficult to weave ivory into mats, the ivory mat, kept in the museum, fully demonstrates the outstanding ingenuity and superb craftsmanship of hte ivory artisans in Guangzhou. Since the making of such ivory mats was very costly, Emperor Yong Zheng decided to ban ivory-mat weaving just for the sake of frugality.

Altogether five ivory mats were made during the reign of Yong Zheng. At present two are still kept in the Palace Museum, one of which is on display in the Treasure Hall.

Illustrations

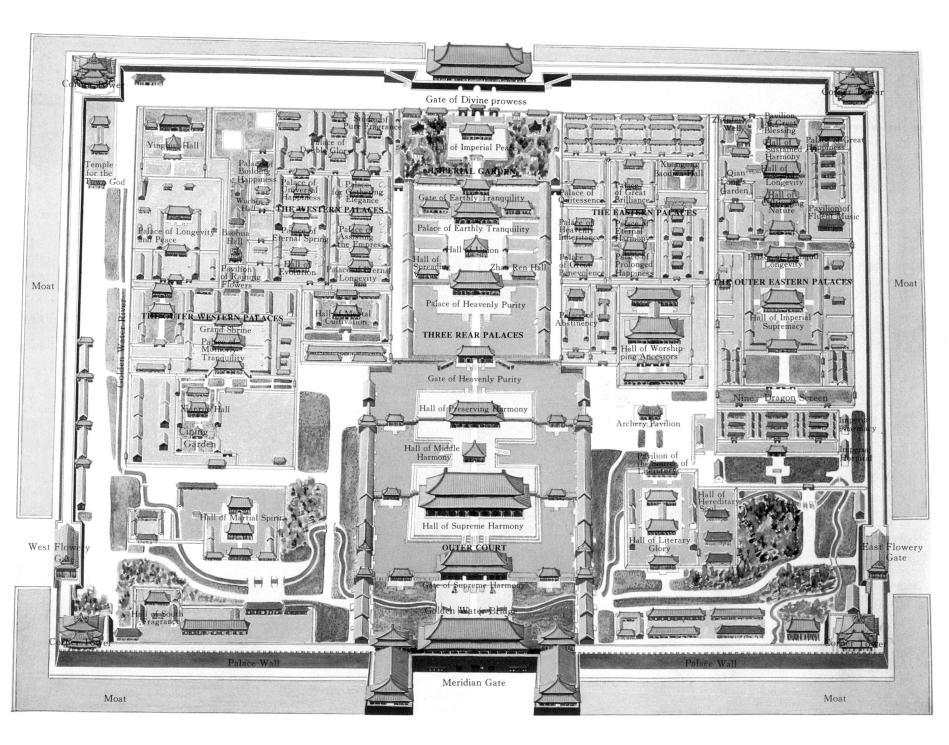

Corner Tower

Gate of Divine prowess

Corner Tower

Temple for the Town God

Yinghua Hall

Studio of Pure Fragrance

Palace of Double Glory

Hall of Imperial Peace

IMPERIAL GARDEN

Zhenfei's Well

Pavilion of Great Blessing

Palace of Great Happiness

Palace of Building Happiness

Hall of Sustained Harmony

Moat

Palace of Universal Happiness

Palace for Gathering Elegance

Gate of Earthly Tranquility

Palace of Quitessence

Palace of Great Brilliance

Xuangong Baodian Hall

Hall of Longevity

Wuchen Hall

THE WESTERN PALACES

Palace of Earthly Tranquility

THE EASTERN PALACES

Qian Long's Garden

Hall of Cultivating Nature

Palace of Longevity and Peace

Baohua Hall

Palace of Eternal Spring

Palace of Assisting the Empress

Hall of Union

Palace of Heavenly Inheritance

Palace of Eternal Harmony

Pavilion of Fluent Music

Hall of Spreading Virtue

Zhao Ren Hall

Pavilion of Raining Flowers

Hall of Evolution

Palace of Eternal Longevity

Palace of Great Benevolence

Palace of Prolonged Happiness

Palace of Tranquil Longevity

Palace of Heavenly Purity

Moat

Hall of Martial Cultivation

THREE REAR PALACES

THE OUTER EASTERN PALACES

THE OUTER WESTERN PALACES

Grand Shrine

Palace of Abstinency

Palace of Motherly Tranquility

Hall of Worshipping Ancestors

Hall of Imperial Supremacy

Xianruo Hall

Gate of Heavenly Purity

Cining Garden

Hall of Preserving Harmony

Nine Dragon Screen

Archery Pavilion

Imperial Pharmacy

Hall of Middle Harmony

Pavilion of the Source of Literancy

Imperial Hospital

West Flowery Gate

Hall of Martial Spirit

Hall of Supreme Harmony

Hall of Hereditary Soul

East Flowery Gate

OUTER COURT

Gate of Supreme Harmony

Hall of Literary Glory

Corner Tower

Hall of South Fragrance

Golden Water Bridge

Corner Tower

Palace Wall

Meridian Gate

Palace Wall

Moat

Moat

Golden Water River

83

Bird's-eye view of the Forbidden City.

The Forbidden City, today called the Palace Museum, stands on the central axis of the capital, running from the Yongding Gate in the south to the Bell-and-Drum Towers in the north. Built between 1406 and 1420 during the reign of Emperor Yong Le of the Ming dynasty, the palace area, 960 meters from north to south and 760 meters from east to west, is surrounded by a 10-meter-high wall and a moat 52 meters wide. The buildings contained 9,999 and a half rooms (today 8,700 still exist). The layout is symmetrical, symbolizing the supreme power of the feudal monarchy, and illustrating the fine traditions and unique style of Chinese architecture.

The wall surrounding the Forbidden City is 3,428 meters long, 10 meters high, 6.66 meters wide at the top and 8.24 meters wide at the bottom. There is a gate on each of the four sides, the Meridian in the south, Shenwu in the north, Donghua in the east and Xihua in the west. Chinese scholar trees and willows encircle the city wall.

Meridian Gate (Wumen), 35.6 meters high, is the south gate. The layout is shaped like the character 凹. Five pavilions tower over the gates, three in the middle and two as side gates. The main pavilion, nine bays wide and five bays deep, is topped by a double-eaved hipped roof. The two square double-eaved pavilions on either side, connected by covered corridors, serve as eastern and western wings of the main pavilion.

East Flowery Gate (Donghuamen), the east gate used by officials coming or going from court duty.

Corner tower of the Forbidden City.

At each of the four corners of the Forbidden City stands a unique tower, each with six hipped and gabled roofs. The three-tiered eaves sloping into 28 upturning curves, together with 10 gables and 72 ridges, add much grace to the structure.

Legend has it that its artisans racked their brains for many days and nights but could not think of an ideal design. Learning this, Lu Ban, the master carpenter of the Spring and Autumn period (770-476 B. C.) descended to the world and walked past the construction site carrying a grasshopper cage in one hand. Inspired, the artisans finally succeeded in building the four corner-towers with supperb workmanship.

The square in front of the Gate of Supreme Harmony. The gate was known as the Fengtian (Mandate of Heaven) Gate in the Ming dynasty and was given its present name in the Qing dynasty. The stream running across the square is known as the Inner Golden Water River and is originated in the Jade Spring Mountain in the western suburb of Beijing. The five carved white marble bridges spanning the stream were the must way to go to the outer court.

珠聯璧合

The Gate of Heavenly Peace (Tiananmen) in Qing dynasty times in the painting "Scenes of Great Joy".

Coal Hill (Jingshan), a natural defence for the Forbidden City.

The moat around the Forbidden city 3,800 meters long, was built duing the Ming dynasty

The former Imperial Palace seen from atop the Coal Hill. Gate of Divine Prowess (Shenwumen), the northern entrance to the Forbidden City, is 31 meters high. During the Qing dynasty candidates of palace maids and palace maids used this gate. The tower above the gate contained a bell and drum. Everyday at dusk the bell would toll 108 times. After that the drum would beat to sound the hour at each watch of the night until the bell again sounded 108 times at sun rise.

Three grand halls in the Outer Court: Hall of Supreme Harmony, Hall of Central Harmony and Hall of Preserving Harmony. They rise on triple-tiered terraces with marble balustrades. They are the most magnificent architecture group in the Forbidden City. Grand ceremonies such as the enthronement, wedding ceremony and birthday celebration of the emperor and the crowning of the empress were held here.

The Hall of Supreme Harmony, popularly known as the Hall of Golden Bells (Jinluandian), rises on a great I-shaped marble terrace along with the Hall of Central Harmony (Zhonghedian) and the Hall of Preserving Harmony (Baohedian). The Hall of Supreme Harmony is 37 meters high, 70 meters wide and 37 meters deep. Its 55-room hall is supported by 72 huge nanmu wood columns. This is the largest ancient wooden structure extant today in China.

The imperial throne and gilded columns entwined with coiled dragons.

The painted golden throne with a splendid screen behind it stands on a two-meter dais in the center of the hall. Flanking the throne are six gilded columns covered with coiled dragons. High above the throne is a magnificent coffered ceiling decorated with dragons playing with pearls. The emperor on this high throne could overlook his subjects in the courtyard below, a position meant to keep them in awe of the Son of Heaven.

Exquisitely patterned imperial throne.

Some of the hall's 72 columns.

The coffered ceiling.

93

Foreign envoys waiting outside the Gate of Supreme Harmony for an audience with the emperor of the Qing Dynasty.

The Hall of Central Harmony (Zhonghedian) and the Hall of Preserving Harmony (Baohedian).

Inside the Hall of Preserving Harmony.

This last of Outer Court buildings is 50 meters wide and 25 meters deep, with a double-eaved, hipped and gabled roof. Here the Qing emperors held banquets and the highest-level examinations to select officials among scholars from all over the country.

"Crowning and Welcoming the Empress Ceremony Held at the Hall of Supreme Harmony in the painting Emperor Guang Xu's Wedding".

Guang Xu's wedding was held on the 27th day of the first lunar month of the 15th year of his reign (1889). The year before, the Empress Dowager Ci Xi had ordered the ceremonies for this event made into a painting.

Ministers saluting in the courtyard of the Hall of Supreme Harmony in the ceremony crowning and welcoming the empress as represented in the painting "Emperor Guang Xu's Wedding".

The bridal sedan chair for the imperial wedding of Emperor Guangxu of the Qing Dynasty.

The Palace of Motherly Tranquility (Cininggong) in Emperor Guang Xu's Wedding.

After the ceremony of crowning and welcoming the empress was over, the groom in ceremonial dress went over to the Palace of Motherly Tranqility to pay his respects to the empress dowager.

The banquet inside the hall was livened up by a court dance performed on the terrace outside—a scene from Emperor Guang Xu's Wedding.

The Hero-Praising Dance shows how eight warriors, symbolizing the Eight Banners, hunted a group of strange beasts with arrows. Then followed another dance performed by ministers and imperial guards inside the hall to celebrate the event.

Bronze crane
outside the hall.

Three-tiered marble terrace with three
flights of stairs leading into the hall.

Along the base of the white marble
balustrade around each tier are 1,142 water-
spouts in the shape of dragon heads. This is a
wondrous spectacle on a rainy day when they
all spurt water.

Bronze tortoise outside the Hall
of Supreme Harmony (Taihedian).

Grain measure in front of
the Hall of Supreme Harmony.

Stone ramp carved with dragons
sporting in the clouds in the center of the
stairway leading down behind the Hall of
Preserving Harmony (Baohedian) to the
courtyard below.

The Pavilion of Manifest Benevolence (Tirenge) stands east of the Hall of Supreme Harmony. Here, following the practice of the Song dynasty emperor Gao Zong, the Qing emperor Kang Xi held special examinations to attract Han intellectuals to his service.

The Pavilion of the Source of Literature (Wenyuange). This imperial library, built in 1774 in the style of the Tianyige Pavilion at Ningbo in Zhejiang province, housed the famous collections *Si Ku Quan Shu* and the *Collected Works from the Past and Present*.

This is the half room of the 9999.5 rooms in the Forbidden City. It is in the western part of the Pavilion of the Source of Literature.

Three Rear Palaces.

Back of the Hall of Preserving Harmony is a horizontal east-west square, the boundary between the inner and outer courts.

103

The Palace of Heavenly Purity (Qianqinggong). Here the emperors resided and dealt with day-to-day affairs of state. There were 27 beds in the Eastern and Western Warm Chambers. This palace was where a court coup d'etat and two unusual cases of treachery took place during the Ming dynasty. Beginning with the Qing emperor Yong Zheng's reign, it became the site for royal family banquets.

The interior of the Palace of Heavenly Purity. The imperial throne is placed on the square platform in the center of the hall. The plaque above the throne says "Justice and Honesty."

A Qing dynasty emperor used to put behind the plaque the box that contained his decree saying who would be the new emperor after his death.

Twenty-five imperial seals of the Qing Emperor Qian Long are kept in the Hall of U-nion (Jiaotaidian).

A bronze water-clock in the hall.

A chiming clock in the Hall of Union.

The Eastern Warm Chamber in the Palace of Earthly Tranquility
served as an imperial bridal chamber in the Qing dynasty.

The bridal bed in the bridal Chamber where the emperor and empress went through their nuptial rite and drank their nuptial wine.

Amber phoenix on the bridal bed. The bed, placed by the south window, was where the emperor and empress drank the nuptial cup. The phoenix was a symbol for happy marriage.

Canopy with a pattern of 100 boys over the wedding bed of the emperor.

110

The west room, where sacrifices were offered to the gods during the Qing dynasty.

Stone base for an army flagpole and the Army Flag God's Temple before the Hall of Imperial Peace (Qin'andian).

The kitchen in the Palace of Earthly Tranquility and two blue-and-white porcelain wine containers.

The flagpole in front of the palace used in worship of the gods.

Petrified wood in front of the House of Crimson Snow (Jiangxuexuan). On it was carved a poem by Emperor Qian Long entitled "Ode to the Petrified Wood".

The Studio for Cultivating Nature (Yangxingzhai). This was used as an imperial library during the reign of Qian Long. Pu Yi, the last Qing emperor, learned English here from a British teacher, Reginald Johnston.

Golden fish in the pond of the Imperial Garden.

Pavilion of a Thousand Autumns (Qianqiuting). Built in the 12th year
of Ming emperor Jia Jing's reign, it contained the memorinl tablet of Emperor Tong Zhi of the Qing dynasty.

Fantastic rock in front of the Tianyimen Gate in the Imperial Garden.

Beijing mockorange trees planted in a square glazed flower bed in front of the House of Crimson Snow during the reign of Dao Guang of the Qing dynasty. Every year in early summer these blossom with fragrant white flowers.

"Zhuge Liang Worshipping the Big Dipper" Rock.

A strangely shaped rock embedded in a carved marble foundation west of the Tianyimen Gate in the Imperial Garden, known for its natural design: an old man in a silk headdress and a purple long-sleeved gown, bowing with both hands clasped in front, seeming to worship the stars in the sky. This coincides with an episode about Zhuge Liang, a statesman and strategist of the Three Kingdoms period (220-265), who was believed to have prayed to the Big Dipper.

The Sun-shading Marquis Tree.

It was a hot summer, legend says, when the Qing emperor Qian Long went south of the Yangtze River. He felt, however, that he was always shaded by a tree. During his absence, a 400-year-old cypress next to Duixiu Hill in the Imperial Garden withered. When he returned, the emperor conferred on it the title "Sun-shading Marquis" and wrote a poem about it.

Duixiu Hill.

In the 11th year of Ming Emperor Wan Li's reign, the Hall of Looking at Flowers (Guanhuadian) was dismantled to build the Duixiu Hill with rocks, with the Pavilion of Imperial Landscape on top of it. Every year at the Double Ninth Festival (the 9th day of the 9th lunar month) the emperor, empress and imperial concubines came to ascend this height.

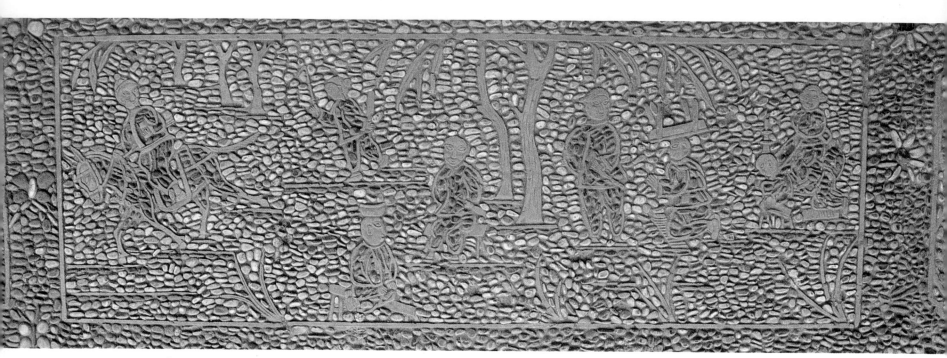

"Henpecked Husbands", also on the cobbled pathway in the Imperial Garden. It depicts two henpecked husbands, one with an oil lamp on his head, kneeling on a wooden bench, the other with a bench on his head, kneeling on a wash board, both being beaten by their wives.

"Horse", worked in stones on the cobbled pathway in the Imperial Garden.

The two-storied Yanhui Pavilion is 15 meters tall, with double eaves.
The cypress in front of the building is hundreds of years old.

Parvilion of Ten Thousand Springs (Wanchunting). Built in the 12th year of the Ming emperor Jia Jing's reign, during the Qing dynasty it contained the portrait of Guan Yu, a general of the Kingdom of Shu during the Three Kingdoms period (220-265), later enshrined as Lord Guan.

117

Qin'an Hall was built in the Ming Dynasty, with an inclined quadrilateral roof. This design is rare in ancient architecture. God of Xuanwu, or Water God, was worshipped in the hall. On the first day of the first lunar month, the emperor worshiped the god here to prevent the palace from fire.

Bird's-eye view of the Western Palaces.

Throne in the Hall of Mental Cultivation. This hall stands south of the Six Western palaces. Eight Qing emperors, from Yong Zheng to Xuan Tong, resided and did their daily work here. Officials who were to be promoted, transferred or whose tenure of office was to expire were presented to the emperor who was seated on this throne.

The the Eastern Warm Chamber of the Hall of Mental Cultivation was where Empress Dowagers Ci Xi and Ci An held court behind the curtain. After the 1861 coup，Ci Xi took supreme power into her own hands and ruled China for 48 years through the reigns of emperors Tong Zhi and Guang Xu.

Framed wall panel with inlaid curio designs.

West room of the Hall of Mental Cultivation, called the Hall of Diligence in Administering State Affairs and Closeness to Worthy Persons. Five emperors of the Qing dynasty, from Yong Zheng to Xian Feng, summoned Privy Council members for audiences here.

The Hall of Happiness (Yanxitang) stands west of the Hall of Mental Cultivation. Ladies of the court, when sent to the emperor's bedroom in proper order, paused for a rest here. It was the residence of Empress Dowager Ci Xi when she served as regent for her son, the child emperor Tong Zhi.

深心託豪素

懷抱觀古今

三希堂

Room of Three Rarities （Sanxitang）

Originally called the Warm Room （Wenshi）, it was renamed the Room of Three Rarities in the 11th year of Qian Long's reign （1746） when three samples of callig- raphy by Wang Xizhi, Wang Xianzhi and Wang Xun, famous calligraphers of the Jin dynasty （265-420） were kept here.

123

The east bedchamber in the hall.

The rear hall was the residence of the Qing emperors. Two of them, Shun Zhi and Qian Long died here.

The Palace for Gathering Elegance.

124

East room in the palace.

Second east room.

The west room: Room of Benevolence and Wisdom.

A section of the bedchamber.

Bed in the west chamber.

Painting "The Goddess Magu Offering Wine" hanging in the Palace of Eternal Spring.

According to legend, Magu, a native of Sichuan, practised yoga in Mount Guyu and became an immortal. On the third day of the third lunar month—believed to be the birthday of the Queen Mother Goddess—Magu made wine with magic fungus on the bank of the Jianghe River to celebrate the event.

Throne for empresses.

East room.

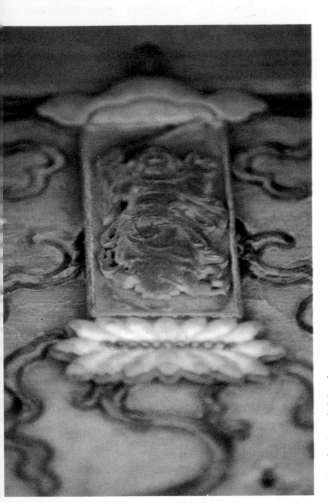

"Lady Feng Barring the Way of a Bear", hanging on the east wall of the Palace of Universal Happiness (Xianfugong).

Feng Yuan was an imperial concubine of Western Han Emperor Yuan Di (reigned 48-33 B. C.). One day the emperor visited a zoo. A bear escaped and rushed to attack the emperor. Feng Yuan ran forward and stood in the animal's way. Her brave deed won the emperor's great respect. The painting, done by Jin Tingbiao, bears inscriptions by Emperor Qian Long.

Portrait of Zhong Kui.

Zhong Kui was believed to be a catcher of demons. His portrait was hung in front of the door of the Palace of Eternal Spring to chase away evil spirits and turn bad luck into good.

Mural "A Dream of Red Mansions in the palace".

Massage instruments made of agate, amber and aventurine were used for empresses and imperial concubines in the Qing court, including Empress Dowager Ci Xi when she sufferd from indigestion.

In the mural a long corridor was done in perspective.

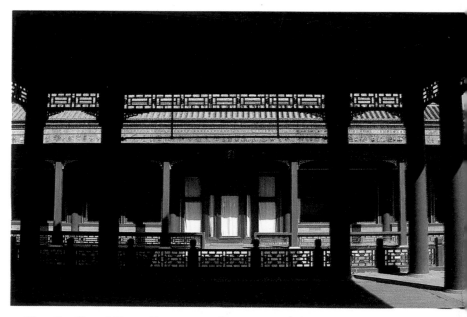

The Studio of Pure Fragrance (Shufangzhai).

131

"Empress Xu Presenting Food", a painting on the east wall of the Palace of Quintessence (Zhongcuigong).

Xu Pingjun, wife of Emperor Xuan Di of the Western Han dynasty (206 B. C. -24 A. D.), came from a humble family. After she was crowned as empress, she continued to lead a frugal life. Every five days, she herself respectfully served food to her mother-in-law.

During the reign of Emperor Qian Long, twelve paintings were made portraying empresses or imperial concubines of ancient times known for their exemplary conduct. These were hung in the east and west palaces every year at Spring Festival.

Curio shelf with many sections of different sizes, where jade objects, gems, jasper, crystals and coral were kept. Most of these were collected during Qian Long's time. The shelf was placed in the imperial bedchambers of the Hall of Mental Cultivation, the Hall for Cultivating Nature, the Palace of Eternal Spring, and the Palace for Gathering Elegance.

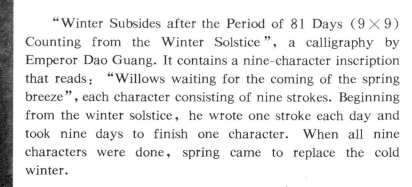

"Winter Subsides after the Period of 81 Days (9 × 9) Counting from the Winter Solstice", a calligraphy by Emperor Dao Guang. It contains a nine-character inscription that reads: "Willows waiting for the coming of the spring breeze", each character consisting of nine strokes. Beginning from the winter solstice, he wrote one stroke each day and took nine days to finish one character. When all nine characters were done, spring came to replace the cold winter.

Framed wall panel with a jadeite-inlaid phoenix design in the bedroom.

The eastern veranda.

The Gate of Tranquil Longevity (Ningshoumen).

The Palace of Tranquil Longevity was first built by Kang Xi, as the rear hall of the present palace. It was reconstructed under Qian Long, the inscribed hall name was moved there over the door. A copy of the Palace of Earthly Tranquility (Kunninggong), the palace was used by the retired emperor to worship Shamanist deities.

The Hall of Imperial Supremacy (Huangjidian).
First known as the Palace of Benevolence and Longevity
(Renshougong) in the Ming times, it was rebuilt under
the Qing emperor Kang Xi and renamed the Palace of
Tranguil Longevity (Ningshougong) as the residence of

his mother. In the 37th year of Qian Long's reign he
received congratulations in the front hall before his
abdication to become retired and changed the name to
the Hall of Imperial Supremacy.

Bird's-eye view of the Hall for Cultivating Nature (Yangxingdian). Modeled after the Hall of Cultivating the Mind, it was the residence of the emperor's father.

West room of this Hall—Room of Fragrant Snow. Inside was an immortals, cave built of quartz where Emperor Qian Long sat to meditate.

The Hall of Joyful Longevity (Leshoutang) stands behind the Palace of Tranquil Longevity and the Hall for Cultivating Nature with the Pavilion of Fluent Music (Changyinge) on the east and Qian Long's Garden on the west. These five form a small "inner court" for the retired emperor.

137

A poem "Western Expedition" by Emperor Qian Long, stored in the Room of Sustained Harmony (Yihexuan). It tells how the Dzungarians, a Mongolian tribe, were quelled in the 23rd year of Qian Long's reign (1758).

Essay "On Dispelling Erroneous Thoughts" by Emperor Qian Long, stored in the Room of Sustained Harmony. It sums up the experience of this expedition.

The Rest-From-Work Studio. There is a small theater stage inside where eunuchs sang arias of Chinese operas by order of Emperor Qian Long.

The Gate of Spreading Prosperity (Yanqimen), the front gate of Qian Long's Garden.

Couplets and tablet inscribed with Qian Long's writing.

Pavilion for Seeking Pleasure during the Purification Ceremony (Xishangting).

The Room of the Rising Sun (Xuhuiting). It faces east and greets the sunrise every morning.

140

The Pavilion of Towering Beauty (Songxiuting).

Hillltop terrace east of the Room of Ancient Glory (Guhuaxuan).

Cup-floating Canal in the pavilion. Wine cups floated along the winding 10-cm.-deep canal cut into the rock floor. In allusion to an essay by a famous Jin dynasty writer Wang Xizhi, Qian Long named the pavilion Xishang—seeking pleasure during the festival held in the spring on river banks to cleanse away evil influences. Surrounded by rockeries on three sides, the pavilion is quiet and tastefully laid out.

The Tower of Living up to Expectations
(Fuwangge), the main building in Qian Long's
Garden. It is also known as the "Ladyrinth"
for its network of winding paths.

The Three Friends Room (Sanyouxuan). Decorations
inside are centered on the theme of the pine, bamboo and
plum—three friends in winter.

The Room for Fulfilling the Original Ideal (Suichutang).

Courtyard of the Room of the Essence of Jade (Yucuixuan).

The Zhuxiang Hall is a storied structure built against a glaze-tiled wall. Inclined corridors flanking both sides of the hall lead to the Yucui and Juanqin studies.

143

Pavilion of Raining Flowers (Yuhuage) seen from afar.

Cave of Clouds (Yundoudong) on the Hill of Taihu Rock east of the Pavilion of Great Blessing (Jingqige). Its name is inscribed in the calligraphy of Emperor Qian Long.

Tiger-skin Wall with a moon gate in the courtyard.

Imperial Concubine Zhen's Well (Zhenfeijing). In 1900 when the Eight-powers Allied Forces reached Beijing, the Empress Dowager Ci Xi, before she fled the capital, had Zhen Fei, Emperor Guang Xu's favorite concubine who supported him in his attempt to carry out reforms, pushed down this well.

Distant view of the Pavilion of Fluent Music.

Pavilion of Fluent Music (Changyinge) built in the 37th year of Qian Long's reign (1772), was the largest theater in the Forbidden City. The 21-meter structure has three stories, each having its own name: Happiness (top), Nobility (middle) and Longevity (lower).

Gallery of the Pavilion for Watching Performances (Yueshilou) where ministers and high officials watched theatrical performances.

The pavilion where the emperor also watched the performances.

The Longevity Platform of the pavilion.

Theater Stage in the studio's courtyard, built during Qian Long's reign. On festive occasions the emperor and ministers would come here to watch performances.

Nine-dragon screen in front of the Gate of Imperial Supremacy (Huangjimen).

Carved ornamental column
at the Gate of Heavenly
Peace (Tiananmen).

Bronze male lion on the east side of the
Gate of Supreme Harmony (Taihemen).

Bronze female lion on the west side.

Gilded bronze mythical beast
(xie zhi) at the Tianyimen Gate.

Gilded bronze unicorn outside the Palace
or Motherly Tranquility (Cininggong).

Gilded bronze elephant
at Chengguangmen Gate.

Bronze phoenix outside the Palace of the Queen Consort (Yikungong).

Sheji Hall. Standing west of the Palace of Heavenly Purity (Qianqinggong), it is a hall of gilded copper, symbol of state power.

Bronze dragon outside the Palace for Gathering Elegance (Chuxiugong).

Gilded bronze vat.

Silence whip. This was cracked three times to command silence when grand ceremonies were about to start. It was wielded by four imperial guards. Then, to strains of music, military and civilian officials knelt and kowtowed to the emperor as he entered and sat on the throne.

Bronze tripod incense burner outside the Hall of Supreme Harmony. A dent on one of its handles was said to have been made by Li Zicheng, leader of the peasant army that captured Beijing and overthrew the Ming dynasty, who wanted to see if his sword was sharp enough.

Dragon-Pillow Stone. Legend says that a golden dragon on top of the Pavilion of Raining Flowers (Yuhuage) slept with this stone as its pillow after drinking water from a jar in the Palace of Eternal Spring (Changchungong).

Jade chimes on the west side of the hall's veranda. Each set consists of 16 chimes of the same size but different thicknesses.

An iron plate with Qing emperor Shun Zhi's imperial edict: "Court eunuchs are not allowed to interfere with government affairs".

Gold chime bells used in court music. These were placed on the east side of the Hall of Supreme Harmony veranda and played at grand ceremonies. Each set consists of 16 gold bells of the same size but of different thicknesses, thus producing different tones.

154

Sundial in front of the Hall of Supreme Harmony (Taihedian).

Details of the sundial in front of the Hall for Cultivating Hature.

Moondial outside the Palace of Motherly Tranguility.

Details of the moondial.

Arrowheads left embedded in the Longzongmen Gate in 1813 by one of the peasant insurgents of the Nature's Law Society (Tianlijiao) who stormed the Forbidden City and fought the Qing troops.

Jiangshan Hall on Wenshi Terrace. It is a hall of gilded copper, symbol of state power.

Willow-branch Stone in the Palace of Earthly Tranquility (Kunninggong). A willow branch inserted into a hole in the stone with the other end tied to a shrine was prayed to for the peace and health of the emperor's son.

Imperialseals of the Qing dynasty.

An imprint of the imperialseal.

Rank marker. This was used to indicate the position where a military or civil official should kneel. During the Qing dynasty, bronze markers replaced the wooden ones used in Ming times. Seventy-two were arranged in two rows on the east and west sides of the imperial road to the Hall of Supreme Harmony, each row consisting of 18 ranks. The marker, 30 cm. high, is hollow inside with an oblate bottom. The rank was indicated in both Manchu and Han languages.

156

Gold ruyi, an S-shaped ornamental object, symbol of good luck.

Ruyi was first referred to in the *History of the Jin Dynasty* (*Jinshu*). By the Qing times it had become a major furnishing in the palace, either beside the throne or in the bedchamber. People gave the ruyi to each other as a gift. Emperor Qian Long was presented 60 gold ones, while the Empress Dowager Ci Xi was given 81, both on their 60th birthday. The emperor would give a ruyi to the empress he had selected.

Accumulated Verdancy in Mount Nanshan, a jade carving in the Hall of Joyful. Longevity (Leshoutang). Its name implies a life as long as that mountain. Carved from a piece of jade weighing 1.5 tons, it took four years to finish in Qian Long's time.

Celestial globe of Qian Long's reign. On the gold spheroid are 300 constellations and 3,240 stars, all inlaid with pearls.

Ivory mat, 216 cm. by 139 cm., of Emperor Yong Zheng's reign.

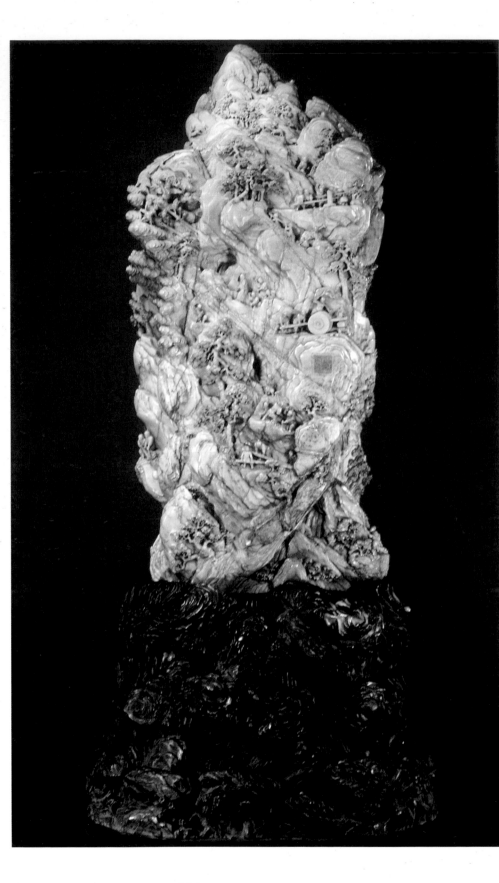

Agate bowl inlaid with gold, Qian Long's reign.

'Yu, the Great Harnessing Floods' is the largest piece of jade carving in China today. This 4,500-kilogram block was quarried in Xinjiang. The inscription on it is in the handwriting of Emperor Qian Long of the Qing Dynasty.

Palace lantern.

Gold goblet. It was used by emperors every New Year Day to drink tusu wine as a preventive against illness during the ceremony for writing the first article of the new year. Inlaid wtth pearls and gems, it is 12. 5 cm. high, 8 cm. around the rim, with three 5-cm. stems. In Chinese the term jin ou (gold goblet) also means territorial integrity and everlasting security.

161

A silver-plated hairpin decorated with red and blue precious stones.

Ming dynasty empress's phoenix crown. Worn in ceremonies by Empress Xiao Duan, wife of Emperor Wan Li, it weighs two kilograms, and is made of gold, kingfisher feathers, more than 100 precious stones and 5,000 pearls.

Qing dynasty empress's phoenix crown worn in summer. Made of black flannel and trimmed with vermilion velvet it has three gold phoenixes on top, one upon another, an important hallmark differentiating the rank of empress from the imperial concubines. The best-preserved of the phoenix crowns worn by Qing dynasty empresses and concubines is decorated with 10 gold phoenixes, a golden longtailed pheasant, eight cat's eyes, 83 eastern pearls from northeast China, and 436 other pearls.

Dragon-Cloud Jar, a jade carving in the Hall of Joyful Longevity (Leshoutang). Its name suggests that happiness is as vast as the Eastern Sea. It was carved from one piece of jade weighing 2.5 tons, and took four years to complete in Qian Long's reign.

Chaozhu (beads worn in court).

Chaozhu was an ornament worn by Qing emperors, empresses, princes, dukes and high officials when they were in ceremonial dress. Each string consists of 108 round beads, signifying the belief that one year was composed of 12 months, 24 solar terms and 72 periods of five days (hou). In between the beads four larger ones represented the four seasons. On the sides were attached three strings of smaller beads, two on the left and one on the right, each of 10 beads representing the first, second and last periods of 10 days in a month. The chaozhu shown here was made of eastern pearls from northeast China and was specially for the use of emperors, empresses and empress dowagers.

Dragon robe for Emperor Qian Long. Embroidered with several-dozen dragons set off by clouds, the sun, the moon, stars, mountains, fire, wine cups etc, it was worn by the emperor in grand ceremonies.

Sleeveless-jacket worn by the empress over her court dress.

Box containing a Qing dynasty emperor's confidential appointment of his successor. It is made of nanmu wood, 32.5 cm. long, 17 cm. wide, and 9cm. high. On the case of yellow felt are nine gilded copper buttons. Characters on the yellow paper strip that sealed the box read: "On the day autumn begins, the 26th year of Dao Guang's reign", and the emperor's signature in Manchu.

Gold hair pagoda. Emperor Qian Long had this pagoda made to keep his mother's hair to show his sad memories and filial piety. The structure is 1.5 meters high and 0.7 meter square at the bottom, and is made of 3,440 taels of gold.

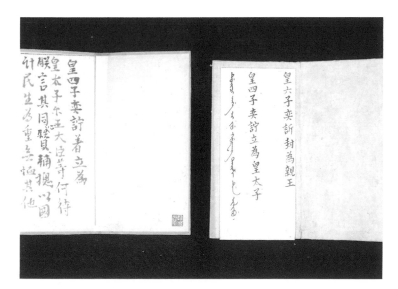

Imperial decree on the appointment of the crown prince written by Emperor Dao Guang in both Manchu and Han languages on the 16th day of the 6th lunar month of the 26th year of his reign.

167

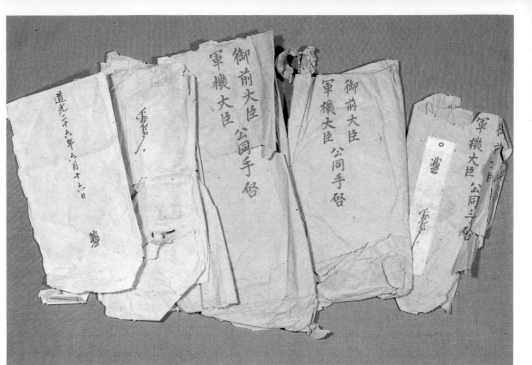

The yellow paper envelope containing this imperial decree on the appointment of the crown prince was addressed to the Privy Council members and other high officials.

Two copies of Dao Guang's last will on the appointment of the crown prince. One was placed in a wooden box，the other kept by the Cabinet.

Menu for Emperor Qian Long, on the sixth day of the sixth lunar month of the 20th year of his reign (1755).

List of successful candidates in the highest-level examinations held in the 33rd year of Kang Xi's reign (1694). It would go to the emperor for his perusal when he received the scholars. at the Hall of Supreme Harmony.

Ming dynasty Emperor Yong Le (1360-1424).

Zhu Di, the third emperor of the Ming dynasty, was the 4th son of Emperor Tai Zu. In the 3rd year of Hong Wu's reign he was made Prince Yan to govern Beiping (modern Beijing). Three decades later he took Nanjing and seized the throne from his nephew Emperor Jian Wen. He ruled for 20 years under the reign title Yong Le.

Qing dynasty Emperor Shun Zhi (1638-1661) .

Aisin-Gioro Fulin, the first emperor of the Qing dynasty, was the 9th son of Emperor Tai Zong. He ascended the throne at six, with his uncle Duoergun as regent. He assumed government duties at 14 and ruled for 18 years under the reign title of Shun Zhi.

Qing dynasty Emperor Kang Xi (1654-1722).

Aisin-Gioro Xuan Ye, the 2nd emperor of the Qing dynasty, was the 3rd son of Emperor or Shun Zhi. He succeeded to the throne at eight with Aobai and some other ministers as regents. He assumed government duties at 12 and ruled for 61 years under the reign title of Kang Xi.

171

Qing dynasty Emperor Qian Long (1711-1799).

Aisin-Gioro Hong Li, 4th son of Emperor Yong Zheng, became the 4th emperor of the Qing dynasty at 25 and ruled for 60 years under the reign title Qian Long. In 1796 he passed the throne to Yong Yan, his 15th son whose reign title was Jia Qing. Qian Long was honored as the "retired father of the emperor".

Qing dynasty Emperor Tong Zhi(1856-1875).

Aisin-Gioro Zai Chun, Edest son of Emperor Xian Feng, ascended the throne at six as the 8th emperor of the Qing court under the reign title Tong Zhi. Empress Dowaggers Ci An and Ci Xi(the emperor's mother) exercised the regency from behind a curtain. At the age of 18 he began his rule in his own name and his reign lasted 13 years.

Two concubines of Qing dynasty Emperor Yong Zheng.

Aisin-Gioro Yin Zhen, 4th son of Emperor Kang Xi, came to the throne at 45 as the 3rd emperor of the Qing dynasty under the reign title Yong Zheng. He ruled for 13 years and died at the age of 57. He had 24 concubines. These two are from the portraits of 12 of them preserved in the Qing palace.

Empress Dowager Ci Xi in standing position.

The two photos were taken in 1903 in the Summer Palace.

Empress Dowager Ci Xi in sitting position.

The Empress Dowager Ci Xi (1835—1908)

Born Yehonala in a Manchu official's family in Shanxi province, she came to the palace in the 2nd year of Emperor Xian Feng's reign. Four years later she bore the emperor a son and the following year was promoted to the highest concubine rank, a position next only to the empress. After the death of Xian Feng at Rehe, her son succeeded to the throne. The mother was given the title of Empress Dowager Ci Xi and, together with the childless Empress Dowager Ci An, reigned behind the curtain after the 1861 coup d'etat. Empress Dowager Ci Xi ruled China for 48 years through the reigns of Tong Zhi and Guang Xu.

This portrait was done by the American painter Kate Carl in 1903 when Ci Xi was 70 years old.

Empress Dowager Ci Xi with Manchu court ladies. Her upper garment is made of 3,500 pearls.

Selected Palace Maids (Xiunü).

According to Qing court regulations, selections of xiunü were made every three years to find concubines for the emperor or wives for princes. Officials of the "Eight Banners" (military-administrative organizations) of the Manchu, Mongol and Han nationalities were obliged to send their daughters between 13 and 17 as candidates.

On the eve of the selection, the candidates would start for the Forbidden City in mule-drawn carriages prepared by themselves. They entered the city through its back gate (Shenwumen, the Gate of Divine Prowess) and waited outside the Shunzhenmen Gate to be selected before the Pavilion of Inducing Splendor (Yanhuige) in the Imperial Garden. Successful candidates could be granted titles of different ranks by the emperor.

Other palace maids were selected every year from among the daughters of the minor officials of the Household Department. The selected palace maids served mainly as attendants for empresses, empress dowagers and imperial concubines.

175

Court eunuchs.

The origin of the eunuch is associated with castration as a form of punishment in ancient China. In Zhou and Qin dynasty times (11th century-207 B. C.) law offenders who had been castrated were often sent to the court to work at odd jobs. The number of eunuchs varied with the dynasties. When the Qing emperor Qian Long was on the throne, there were 2,666 eunuchs.

Namelist of Xiunü.

Namelist of junior eunuchs.

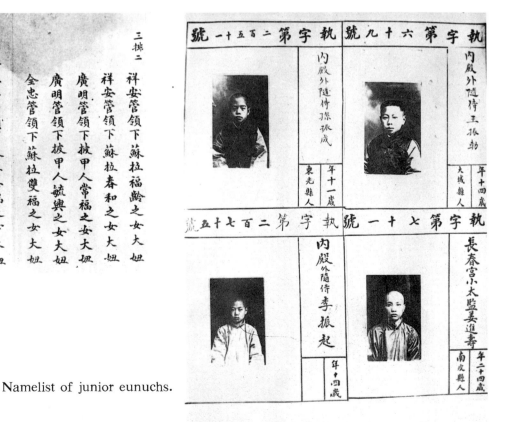

Four famous eunuchs in the late Qing Dynasty. From right: Zhang Haiting, Liu Xingqiao, Wang Fengchi, and Yang Zizhen.

Eunuchs at work.

An elder palace maid and two yong palace maids.

A palace maid.

178

Qing dynasty Emperor Xuan Tong (1906-1967).

Aisin-Gioro Pu Yi, eldest son of Prince Chun. was the last emperor of the Qing dynasty. He came to the throne at the age of three and ruled for three years under thr reign title Xuan Tong. He was dethroned after the revolution of 1911 broke out.

APPENDIX I : EMPERORS

Reign Title	Honorary Title	Posthumous Title	Name	Date of Birth	Date of Coronation
Hong Wu	Ttai Zu	Gao	Zhu Yuanzhang	Oct. 21, 1328	Jan. 23, 1368
Jian Wen		Gongminhui	Zhu Yunwen	Dec. 5, 1377	June 30, 1398
Yong Le	Cheng Zu	Wen	Zhu Di	May 14, 1360	July 17, 1402
Hong Xi	Ren Zong	Zhao	Zhu Gaozhi	Aug. 16, 1378	Sep. 7, 1424
Xuan De	Xuan Zong	Zhang	Zhu Zhanji	Feb. 25, 1398	June 27, 1425
Zheng Tong Tian Shun	Ying Zong	Rui	Zhu Qizhen	Nov. 29, 1427	Feb. 7, 1435 Feb. 11, 1457
Jing Tai	Dai Zong	Jing	Zhu Qiyu	Sep. 21, 1428	Sep. 22, 1449
Cheng Hua	Xian Zong	Chun	Zhu Jianshen	Dec. 9, 1447	Feb. 27, 1464
Hong Zhi	Xiao Zong	Jing	Zhu Youtang	July 30, 1470	Sep. 22, 1487
Zheng De	Wu Zong	Yi	Zhu Houzhao	Oct. 26, 1491	June 19, 1505
Jia Jing	Shi Zong	Su	Zhu Houcong	Sep. 16, 1507	May 27, 1521
Long Qing	Mu Zong	Zhuang	Zhu Zaihou	Mar. 3, 1537	Feb. 4, 1566
Wan Li	Shen Zong	Xian	Zhu Yijun	Sep. 4, 1563	July 19, 1572
Tai Chang	Guang Zong	Zhen	Zhu Changluo	Aug. 28, 1582	Aug. 28, 1620
Tian Qi	Xi Zong	Zhe	Zhu Youxiao	Dec. 23, 1605	Sep. 28, 1620
Cong Zhen	Si Zong	Min	Zhu Youjian	Feb. 6, 1611	Oct. 2, 1627

OF THE MING DYNASTY

Age at Coronation	Years on the throne	Date of Death	Years of Life	Burial Place
41	31	June 24, 1398	71	Shenlie Mountain, Nanjing
22	4	July 13, 1402	26	
43	22	Aug. 12, 1424	65	Changping county, Beijing
47	1	May 29, 1425	48	Changping county, Beijing
28	10	Jan. 31, 1435	38	Changping county, Beijing
9 1 (re-cornated)	22	Feb. 23, 1464	38	Changping county, Beijing
22	8	Mar. 14, 1457	30	Jinshan Mountain, Beijing
18	23	Sep. 9, 1487	41	Changping county, Beijing
18	18	June 8, 1505	36	Changping county, Beijing
15	16	Apr. 20, 1521	31	Changping county, Beijing
15	45	Jan. 23, 1567	60	Changping county, Beijing
30	6	July 5, 1572	36	Changping county, Beijing
10	48	Aug. 18, 1620	58	Changping county, Beijing
39	29 day	Sep. 26, 1620	39	Changping county, Beijing
16	7	Sep. 30, 1627	23	Changping county, Beijing
18	17	Apr. 25, 1644	35	Changping county, Beijing

APPENDIX II :   EMPERORS OF

Reign Title	Honorary Title	Posthumous Title	Name	Date of Birth	Date of Coronation
Tian Ming	Tai Zu	Gao	Nurhachi	1559	Feb. 17, 1616
Tian Cong Cong De	Tai Zong	Wen	Huangtaiji	Nov. 28, 1592	oct. 20, 1626
Shun Zhi	Shi Zu	Zhang	Fu Lin	Mar 15, 1638	Oct. 8, 1643
Kang Xi	Sheng Zu	Ren	Xuan Ye	May. 4, 1654	Feb. 17, 1661
Yong Zheng	Shi Zong	Xian	Yin Zhen	Dec. 13, 1678	Dec. 27, 1722
Qian Long	Gao Zong	Chun	Hong Li	Sep. 25, 1711	Oct. 18, 1735
Jia Qing	Ren Zong	Rui	Yong Yan	Nov. 13, 1760	Feb. 9, 1796
Dao Guang	Xuan Zong	Cheng	Wen Ning	Sep. 16, 1782	Oct. 3, 1820
Xian Feng	Wen Zong	Xian	Yi Zhu	July. 17, 1831	Mar. 9, 1850
Tong Zhi	Mu Zong	Yi	Zai Chun	Apr. 27, 1856	Nov. 11, 1861
Guang Xu	De Zong	Jing	Zai Tian	Aug. 12, 1871	Feb. 25, 1875
Xuan Tong			Pu Yi	Feb. 7, 1906	Dec. 2, 1908

THE QING DYNASTY

Age of Coronation	Years on the Throne	Date of Death	Years of Life	Burial Place
58	11	Sep. 30, 1626	68	Tianzhu Mountain, Shenyang
35	17	Sep. 21, 1643	52	Longyue Mountain, Shenyang
6	18	Feb. 5, 1661	24	Zunhua county, Hebei
8	61	Dec. 20, 1722	69	Zunhua county, Hebei
45	13	Oct. 8, 1735	58	Yixian county, Hebei
25	60	Feb. 7, 1799	89	Zunhua county, Hebei
37	25	Sep. 2, 1820	61	Yixian county, Hebei
39	30	Feb. 25, 1850	69	Yixian county, Hebei
20	11	Aug. 22, 1861	31	Zunhua county, Hebei
6	13	Jan. 12, 1875	19	Zunhua county, Hebei
4	34	Nov. 14, 1908	38	Yixian county, Hebei
3	3	Oct. 17, 1967	61	

AFTERWORD

The Forbidden City in Beijing published in Chinese was warmly received by scholars at home and abroad, selling to the United States, Britain, France, Germany, Japan, Hongkong, Taiwan, countries in Southeast Asia and many other places. The album with more than 200,000 Chinese characters and 265 illustrations, introduces systematically the Outer Court, Inner Court, the Palace for the Supersovereign, the Palace for the Empress Dowager, cultural relics attached to the palace, lives of the emperor, the empress, male and female servants.

We publish this album in English to meet the demands of many readers. The translation was done by Professor Gu Shilong of China International Travel Service, Professor Fu Xukun of Beijing Chemical Industry Institute, Editor-in-Chief Ye Jin of the *Globe* magazine of Xinhua News Agency and senior translator Cui Sigan of *China Pictorial*. The English text was edited by famous translator Yang Xianyi, language specialist Robert Friend of the United States and Liu Zongren of China Today Press.

The photos were provided by Wang Hui of *Outlook* magazine of Xinhua News Agency, Liu Chen of *China Today* magazine, and Hu Chui and Zong Tongchang of Beijing Palace Museum. The maps of the Forbbiden City were drawn by Shen Yunrui of China Youth Press. The designer of the album is technical editor Gao Zongren of China Today Press.

Authors

Februray 1993, Beijing